THE HOUR OF THE FOX

THE HOUR OF THE FOX

Tropical Forests, the World Bank,
and Indigenous People in Central India

Robert S. Anderson and Walter Huber

UNIVERSITY OF WASHINGTON PRESS

Seattle and London

For the people of Bastar

For Hermy Huber

For Kathy Mezei

Copyright © 1988 by the University of Washington Press
Composition by J. Whaley, Computing Services, Simon Fraser University
Printed in the United States of America

Library of Congress Cataloguing-in-Publication Data

Anderson, Robert S.
    The hour of the fox : tropical forests, the World Bank, and indigenous people in Central India / Robert S. Anderson and Walter Huber
      p. cm.
    Bibliography: p.
    Includes index.
    ISBN 0-295-96603-3
    1. Forestry projects—India—Bastar (District) 2. World bank.
  I. Huber, Walter. II. Title.
SD646.B37A53 1988
333.75'15'09543—dc19
                                      87-32290
                                        CIP

IN THE TIME of transition between day and night, say Bastar's tribal people, lies "the hour of the fox." In this twilight hour, when monsoon rains often diminish into mist, they say the elusive fox can be glimpsed silently slipping through the forest.

These are also times of transition for the people—not only is the annual monsoon the fertile season for the forest, but now also the entire people-forest relationship is undergoing great change. The hour of the fox has become a poignant and unpredictable time. What is the collective future of the fox, the people, and the forest? To the people, the fox is a sign, a sign of intimate knowledge of the forest and of freedom to interact intricately with it. To the people, the hour of the fox is very important. In a new era of pine plantations, in a vastly simplified ecology stretching for miles and miles, where would the fox belong? And where would the people belong?

Contents

Illustrations

Maps

Photographs, following page 50

Preface

THIS BOOK evolved in discussions over many years. Having lived and studied for long periods in India, we later discovered a common interest in the development of forestry in Bastar. Between 1978 and 1985 Huber made a number of journeys to Bastar for fieldwork and completed an academic thesis. Anderson also made a visit to Bastar and the forestry project. In addition to this first-hand observation, we conducted lengthy discussions and interviews with tribal leaders, environmentalists, development and banking officials, journalists, local foresters and international consultants, and politicians and government officers—in India and elsewhere. We also analyzed a number of unpublished documents. There is information we have not seen, but we think it timely to present our story now because of its importance in illustrating a worldwide pattern.

This is a contentious subject. Some people were enthusiastic about our work; others were, to put it mildly, cautious. But everyone was curious. How could such an ambitious project be brought to a halt? Were there viable alternatives? It is testimony to the importance of the inquiry that we received so much cooperation from so many quarters, despite potential for political repercussion. We have honored the numerous requests for anonymity, naming only those sources or respondents who had already published on an aspect of this subject. Nevertheless our knowledge is direct, and we are indebted to certain unacknowledged individuals during and following completion of the manuscript.

Bastar has become an increasingly closed place. Because the expectation of resource extraction is so high and the potential for public and private profit is so large, the spirit of investigation has been severely constricted. Playing for high stakes encourages roughness. Despite this, many of our unnamed sources in Bastar and elsewhere in India felt that their information was crucial. They were relieved that someone could translate it into the bigger drama we recount here.

During the project's planning and development, dozens of people came from other parts of India, and from other countries, to work in Bastar—people who would otherwise have had no reason to come. They learned a great deal about Bastar's forests and people. Some of them spoke to us about the deep impact Bastar's conditions had made on them. With feeling, and sometimes with passion, they described the complexity of the project and their concerns about the role of the tribal people. (Even those who expected that a harmonious fit would ultimately be achieved between tribal life and the project were themselves convinced that such a fit was strongly called for.)

This book acknowledges what these visitors learned about Bastar—and their deep concerns. We do not know what shape their concerns might have taken had the project proceeded. But clearly the tribal people and others in Bastar learned very little about these outsiders and their expertise. The forest-dwellers' knowledge of the forest was largely disregarded. The accumulation of knowledge and experience (and income) through the project was profoundly unequal. This book shows how such inequality—and the project's disregard for tribal people—had practical consequences.

We must note that, in Bastar and throughout India, indigenous people are termed "tribal." This term has bureaucratic origins and has been entrenched in the Indian Constitution, with ministries and departments of tribal development and seats in Parliament reserved for tribal people. The term is used, when necessary, by the indigenous people themselves. It carries less and less pejorative value, but only insofar as the additional qualifiers "primitive" or "backward" have been eroded by the deliberate impositions of assimilation. In Bastar in the 1970s and 1980s, it distinguishes 1.44 million people from the 400 thousand nontribals organized in Hindu castes or as members of other major groups, like Muslims or Sikhs. Although some of these latter have lived in Bastar for up to four hundred years, they are not considered indigenous in terms of Indian society. The significance of this distinction is examined below in its appropriate context.

Every effort was made to have the manuscript read by experts in various subjects of the book. Anonymous readers made excellent suggestions. They indeed strengthened the book, and we are very grateful. At the invitation of Paul Brass of the University of Washington, we also presented the results of our work to the South Asia Conference of the Pacific Northwest (SACPAN). SACPAN maintains a delightful twenty-year-old tradition of regular academic interchange between Seattle and Vancouver, and the critique given to us there was both trenchant and encouraging. We thank Professor Brass for his consistent encouragement toward publication of this work, and SACPAN for being a continuing forum of well-informed debate about South Asia. We acknowledge with genuine gratitude the work of Lynne Hissey, who aided us so skillfully in the book's final stages; and of Amparo Cadavid, Maureen Hole, and James Pratt in preparing the manuscript, Lucie Menkveld and Cheryl Chang in typing it, Tirthankar Bose for some of the translations, and Margaret Wheat for the cartography. At Simon Fraser University's Computing Services both Margaret Sharon and Ellen Sangster provided essential assistance including setting the book in type. Excellent advice and encouragement were given to us by Naomi Pascal, Julidta Tarver, and Gretchen Swanzey at the University of Washington Press. A grant from Simon Fraser University's Publication Fund helped to bring this book into print, and the generous assistance of the librarians of Simon Fraser University and the University of British Columbia was an invaluable contribution to its completion.

We also acknowledge the inspiration of our teachers, Milton Singer and Bernard Cohn at the University of Chicago, and Ken Burridge and Michael Ames at the University of British Columbia. Finally we record the courage and tenacity of Sharad Chandra Verma of Bastar, district historian and journalist, who discussed many of these issues with us, and wrote about them for the Indian public.

Robert S. Anderson   Walter Huber
Simon Fraser University   Tokyo
Burnaby, B.C., Canada

October 1987

THE HOUR OF THE FOX

CHAPTER 1

Introduction: Bastar and the Problem of Tropical Forests

SINCE 1984 almost everyone has heard of Bhopal. Its name now symbolizes sudden industrial disaster, sweeping all other headlines away, killing and injuring thousands. That chemical plant was built in Bhopal because of international calculations of increased demands put upon agriculture in the 1960s—the green revolution. Not far from Bhopal, in the 1960s and 1970s, a huge forest plantation was being planned for Bastar—spurred by international calculations of increased demands put upon tropical forestry. The likelihood of sudden disaster here was low: destruction by fire would take a week; by pest attack, months. The consequences of this project, nevertheless, could have been profound.

Here, in the huge district of Bastar, great changes were planned, largely out of sight of Bhopal. The project, which proposed to transform an enormous section of India's largest forest area to a plantation containing one species of pine, was implemented in 1975. Based on years of planning by the world's forestry experts, the project was predicated on major changes in the biological, sociological, and legal environments. In this sense, it differed little from other large-scale industrial schemes intended to transform backward Third World regions and to deal with the problem of national balance of payments. For eighty years, dreamers and schemers had viewed Bastar (the largest forest district in India, the size of Belgium) as a potential El Dorado—"the Ruhr of the East."

Although the World Bank, the Indian government, and a newly created forestry corporation expected elements of risk in the project and

3

knew that the indigenous tribal people living in the forest might not cooperate, little scientific attention was paid to the conditions or views of these "backward" tribal people. Their views and conditions, however, were probably decisive in the unexpected termination of the project in 1981. In addition to unresolved technical issues (pine-plantation growth rates, land use, pulp and paper mill organization, public and private investment), the indifference—and later hostility—of these tribal people reverberated to the top of the political system. Distressed by outside political interference in the tribal kingdom (including the killing of their king), and under the influence of a messianic prophet during the evolution of the industrial forestry project, the tribal people developed resistance to commercial penetration of their forest. Moreover, confrontations have occurred before, and they will probably occur again.

This book, then, assesses the assumptions of the biological, sociological, and legal changes envisaged in the project: the empirical depth of international development as applied to industrial plantation forestry stands in sharp contrast with the shallow approach to the question of tribal people present in the forest. This question turns out to be surprisingly important. This book argues for a realistic theory of natural resource development, special communication responsibilities in projects involving aboriginal people, and increased public benefits (both local and national) from World Bank–funded projects. Because such conflicts are prevalent in many parts of the world, lessons from this situation have a wide applicability. Conclusions can be drawn about opportunities missed and responsibilities unfulfilled by the World Bank and by the state and central governments in India. Little of lasting public value remains after the huge expenditure. Particularly empty is the fund of scientific knowledge which might have been generated. Planners and developers of projects must overcome the striking contradiction between their technical sophistication and their social naivete, particularly in regard to involvement of and communication with indigenous people.

Tropical deforestation is a major problem that needs clarifying. Tropical forests support complex ecological chains while playing an essential and salutary role in the earth's climate and atmosphere. They can return as much as 75 percent of the moisture they receive to the atmosphere. Thus they have a profound effect on rainfall. Yet these vast forests, surrounded by the world's greatest populations, are being rapidly diminished for the immediate needs of those populations. In addition, the activity of international forestry corporations operating in world markets is putting an even greater strain on the tropical jungles and forests. It is uncommon, however, to be shown precisely how deforestation occurs. All too often the process is obscured. But in the short life of the Bastar forestry project, all the players and all the elements constituting the problem of tropical forests were brought onto center stage. The players took these elements and enacted a drama now being played out in many parts of the world.

The problem of tropical forests is defined differently by the people who live in the forests and by all the other peoples who expect to use the trees. The players included the 1.84 million people living in Bastar district, central and state government officials in the district, members of a state forestry development corporation created for World Bank investment, planners and politicians in Bhopal, New Delhi, and Washington, D.C., and scientific experts around the world. What are the elements of the drama? Turning a complex forest into a genetically simplified plantation is basic to the story. Commercial forestry has been penetrating Bastar's forests for seventy years, and various local tribal (and nontribal) groups have been forced to adapt to this penetration. Citizens of their own legendary kingdom, the tribals have slowly become special second-class inhabitants of one of the world's largest nations. Their kingdom is now governed by a new type of outsider who administers the exploitation of the forest and the economic development of the district. Throughout this process, the tribals have searched for new forms of leadership in a variety of attempts to revive their political life and their relationship with the forest.

The government officials, including the historic Forest Departments of the central and state governments, were joined in this project by a brand-new financial, technical, and political vehicle—a forestry development corporation. Together, they were expected to approach the problem of tropical forests in a fresh manner. This approach was planned by various experts in India and abroad who interpreted the problem on a continental and even a global scale. The Bastar project for them was one of many. Its termination was disappointing to some, considering all their work. But most of them had alternatives. The people of Bastar had no other forests.

Point of view influences the significance of any development project. For the forestry corporation, the consulting firms, and the forestry division of the World Bank, the termination of the Bastar project in 1981 was final. Enormous inertia would have to be overcome to revive a forestry project of this scale. But from the point of view of the tribal people of Bastar, the pine project would be replaced by other projects. For them, the forestry project had been just one in a series of interventions by outsiders. Had we examined development in Bastar in the 1960s, the focus might have been on a large iron ore mine and its railway to the coast. Earlier, it would have been on eucalyptus plantations or sawmills supplied by trucks. In the near future, it might be on a cement factory and hydroelectric dams. Neither Bastar's internal development nor its relations with the outside world stands or falls on the termination of a single project, even one of such magnitude as the pine project. But the persistence of the view of Bastar as "El Dorado" or "Ruhr of the East" has guaranteed a succession of outside projects, largely unconnected to one another. The people of Bastar, however, might well connect these projects, looking to each one for opportunities even while fearing cumulative effects and successive failures.

None of the groups of players—whether tribal people or development bankers—spoke with one voice during this drama. There were no puppets, no memorized scripts. The problems facing each of the groups had a variety of interpretations, as did the terms they used. For example, to the corporation, a "tree" was a resource to be mined for cash flow and replaced; to the forest department, it was capital to be reserved and protected from tribals; and to bankers and planners, it was a substitute for other trees as sources of paper. To outsiders, the forest was an "environment." To the tribal people, it was their "place," their home. Even within each group, people took slightly different positions on basic questions.

As a dramatic adventure, the project was guided by expertise. The experts called in by the World Bank and the Government of India to plan and implement the project were required to interpret it in terms of its possible use of new technologies and processes (e.g., the blending of pine and bamboo fibers, the growing of pine in Bastar, the use of Earth Resources Technology Satellite photography for resource planning). They were also to calculate requirements for workers, wood, water, and so forth. All of the sophistication and gadgetry of the applied sciences in silviculture, economics, or process engineering were evident. Interpretation of the project's impact upon forest people was subordinated to these other technical requirements, or "entailments."

The current uses of the forest and the underlying disagreements about rights to such uses were noted but were not empirically studied. The interests of forest people, tribal and nontribal, were also "technical," but the applied sciences in this project had their own hierarchy, supported by the development bankers. Tribal people were low on this hierarchy, as was shown by the budget (see table 1). The problem of tropical forests would mean something different, after all, to silviculturists, economists, and anthropologists. But while experts have continued to differ, time is running out. Science knows less about the tropical forest than other environments, and the tropical forest is disappearing at a greater rate than other environments.

What is the central problem of tropical forests? What other problems are its natural allies? The main problem lies essentially in the value of the forests when compared with the current rate of their disappearance. Their value to humans, of course, lies in their common characteristics, and their disappearance is owing to their vulnerability.

Tropical forests characteristically contain a vast range of animal species and plant varieties, a biological diversity of extraordinary genetic value to the ecosystems into which humans must fit. These species and varieties, packed densely into niches, are historically much older than those of temperate climate forests. The high temperatures and humidity in the tropical forests, coupled with heavy rainfall, have created complex systems that interact in many ways still mysterious to scientists. Their diversity, density, and complexity are important, but their coherence above all gives them their tendency toward equilibrium. The forest canopy traps some of the heavy rainfall, and although the soil itself tends to be leached out and to be rather poor in nutrients, nutrients exist in the biomass covering the forest floor and its root systems. It is therefore important, for example, to trace the activities of fungi like mycorrhizae which enable the absorption of nutrients and water into root systems.

The tropical forests relate significantly to world climates and atmosphere: they return a high percentage of moisture to the atmosphere, thus making essential contributions to regular rainfall. Where the forest disappears, there is usually less regular rainfall via transpiration. The

TABLE 1
Bastar Forestry Project Budget, 1976–1980
(Items ranked in order of size, in thousand U.S. dollars)

	Local	Foreign	Total
1. Pilot Plantations	2,950	337	3,287
2. Price Contingencies	1,498	529	2,027
3. Feasibility Study	860	815	1,675
4. Pilot Logging / Training	365	54	419
5. Research Trials	206	25	231
6. Physical Contingencies	131	44	175
7. Site Assessment Survey	137	35	172
8. Specialists / Studentships	13	111	124
9. Study on Tribals	100	–	100
TOTAL	6,260	1,950	8,210

Financing Plan:

India, Government of Madhya Pradesh	3,500
World Bank	4,000
subtotal	7,550
Madhya Pradesh Forestry Development Corporation	660
total	8,210

(all foreign funds to be a direct grant to MPFDC)

Source: IBRD / IDA Report No. P–1733–IN, Annex, Ill., December 1975.
Note: The Bastar TAP was extended through 1981 by the World Bank. The subtotal shown is $50,000 more than the correct figure of $7,500,000. This error is in the Bank's original calculations in its documents.

affected area often experiences higher temperatures. People in Bastar have noted these effects of deforestation (less rain and higher temperatures) and believe them to be related to deforestation although there are no historic data available in Bastar. In the tropics, temperatures and rainfall regimes are critical mainstays to huge human populations.

The human societies that inhabit or surround tropical forests could not survive without them. The forests provide fuels, building materials, clothes, medicines, cosmetics, beverages—indeed, a multitude of treasures known to the tribal and nontribal people who live there. Their lives are inextricably bound with the forests in practice and in meaning. Also bound are the herds of animals, flocks of birds, swarms of insects—all contributing to a dynamic equilibrium. The rate of the forests' disappearance, therefore, constitutes a problem not only for tribal people but for distant bankers. The Bastar project is but one element in a drama played out in many parts of the world.

The actual velocity of deforestation in tropical forests is very difficult to calculate, even with the LANDSAT satellites. LANDSAT 4 has provided two and one half times the power of detailed documentation of its predecessor, LANDSAT 3. Nonetheless, it cannot pick out small plots of forest clearings made by forest farmers. The total impact of human activities on the forests is sometimes termed "conversion." This controversial term seems to carry an ideological load, dividing forestry experts and professionals in the same manner as demographic forecasts. For some people, the term "conversion" carries alarmist implications of a wood famine; for others, it simply denotes the sum of all cutting, degradation, and elimination of forests. There are large differences in estimates of conversion rates. A University of Washington study, commissioned by the U.S. Department of State, reports that in 1981 the overall rate of conversion of tropical forests was 72,670 square kilometers per year. At this rate, it would require 165 years to convert all closed tropical forests (as long as converted land would not revert back to forest).[1] At the same time, calculations made by the United Nations Food and Agriculture Organization (FAO) and the United Nations Environmental Program showed that the rate of complete deforestation in 1980 was 76,000 square kilometers per year of "tropical forest resources."[2] These calculations differed from those of Norman Myers for the U.S. National Academy of Sciences, or from those of the Global 2000 studies, which predicted disappearance of tropical forests by the year 2020. Myers estimated, at the time the Bastar project was terminated, that conversion by destruction and degradation was affecting 256,000 square kilometers per year (i.e., 20,500 km^2 converted by cattle ranchers, 28,500 km^2 by commercial forestry, and 207,000 km^2 by forest farmers).[3] This is equivalent to an area the size of Yugoslavia. This rate, said the University of Washington study, was much higher than they felt the FAO data indicated. Myers later revised his calculations to include 1983 data. He arrived at 200,000 square kilometers of primary forest being "significantly converted" every year—recognizing that conversion patterns were highly differentiated. Myers then reviewed the same data to arrive at a total figure of 92,000 square kilometers for annual outright elimination of tropical forests.[4] At this later stage United Nations agencies decided on an area the size of Portugal or Austria—smaller than Yugoslavia, but still very significant—as a figure for conversion.

All of these conversion velocity estimates, ranging from 72,000 to 92,000 square kilometers, were extrapolated from incomplete data. Although the first FAO survey of tropical forests occurred in 1948, only 35 percent of Asian forests had been studied by 1985, with even fewer on other continents. In a country like India, the data base was scattered. "In fact," said the FAO in 1981, "no comprehensive study of forest resources or forest land for the entire country [of India] has ever been done."[5] Moreover, the situation in any particular forest was unclear and could be misleading: in a district of neighboring Uttar Pradesh state, according to official figures, 67 percent of the area was covered by forests. Satellite images, however, revealed the true figure to be 37.5 percent.[6] Some of these differences stemmed from foresters' disputed definitions of what should qualify as a forest, whether monocultural plantations of eucalyptus and pine should be included (of which there were 110,000 km^2 in the tropics), and what should constitute conversion.

Despite the differences among these studies of conversion, all have pointed to the dramatic consequences of deforestation, and the need to examine its principal causes. In addition to human activities, tropical forests have been vulnerable to volcanoes, fires, droughts, hurricanes, and typhoons. When the forest disappears, the very poor soils support scrub and weeds, but little else. Heavy rainfall beats with its greatest force upon the open ground, causing massive erosion, and conveying good soils as silt and sedimentation through the rivers, thereby changing the nature and the chemistry of the rivers. In practical terms, the reservoirs of dams built for hydroelectricity silt up at a surprising rate. Deforestation also causes devastating floods. The exposed earth heats to higher temperatures with conversion, and it is debated whether rainfall has, in specific areas, been reduced. Conversion by burning the forest's carbon mass contributes further to the accumulation of CO_2 in the atmosphere; although these forecasts are controversial, some experts contend that this increased CO_2 will accelerate the greenhouse effect, trapping reradiation and thus increasing the overall global temperatures. The fundamental role of the forests is clear:

> When net production of seasonal and wet tropical forests are combined, their total organic matter production and also CO_2 utilization are greater than for the open ocean, which covers 60 percent of the world surface (the tropical forests cover 11 percent of continental land mass).[7]

Deforestation thus contributes to increases in atmospheric CO_2 by reduction of the photosynthetic base and by burning of the forest components. Widespread forest-burning in the tropics can be seen in satellite photographs. Greater CO_2 levels may increase photosynthetic efficiency and aid food production, and higher temperatures may compensate for earth's cooling trends. Conversely, speculates the University of Washington study, the irreversible warming of oceans may trigger the release of even more CO_2 from the oceans, fundamentally altering the temperature and precipitation patterns.

Of course, tribal people in North America and elsewhere have cut and burned patches in the forest to cultivate gardens or to attract big game; historically, they have moved on. These activities were included in the annual conversion rate for forest farmers: the patches burned were not large in proportion to the total land these tribal people used extensively for shifting cultivation.

After conversion, the attempt by some commercial farmers to fertilize the poor forest soils tends to kill fungi and microorganisms beneficial to the forest root systems, further depleting the soils. There is also an experimental "edge effect"; the ecological richness along the cutting edge declines, the way wood rots first at its cut edges. Every living thing changes with deforestation; the human societies in and around tropical forests change too—although not from this cause alone.[8] Ecological conversion occurs along with biological conversion. Deforestation is total, not because almost all the valuable trees are removed, but because the process destroys the coherence of the forest system. What remains is both dwarfed and skewed.

The global problem of tropical forests contains within it a series of component problems. These problems, also evident in the Bastar project, involve issues of tropical forestry, tribal people's development, wildlife, and firewood. Each problem interacts with the others; no aspect is independent. They are presented here just as they were defined and communicated throughout the international system during the Bastar project period, and just as they were described to us in expert discussions. Such definitions do not exist only in documents.

The problem of tropical forestry greatly concerned the planners of the Bastar project. For them, the issue lay in their perception that tropical forests had low productivity and contributed little to gross national product (GNP) or to government revenue in comparison with the land area occupied. Forests also contributed little to the foreign exchange earnings of most countries, and too great an amount of scarce foreign exchange was being spent on importing forest products (papers, etc.). Moreover, a disproportionately small percentage of the work force of developing countries gained formal employment in forestry. To tribal people, however, the problem of tropical forestry centered on its increasing penetration of their domain. Its commercial scale dwarfed the petty traders, small mills, and slightly mechanized labor gangs with which they once dealt. The development planners have defined the problem so as to admit one solution—the higher rate of conversion now under way by forest corporations. This means intensive and industrial-scale utilization of existing forests; it means their replacement by plantations of one or two species.

To development planners, the problem of tribal people lies in the fact that commercially attractive tropical forests are now in less accessible regions, into which the tribal people themselves historically (as described below) have been pushed. These people now inhabit or surround forests. Beneath their feet also lie mineral or petroleum resources now of great value to governments and corporations. Unless public or private forces are used to clear the tribal presence off this land and out of the forests, planners must account for them and must invent ways to exclude them from or engage them in projects. This has varied from project to project. For example, in Canada new uranium mines in northern Saskatchewan enrolled more than half of their labor force from the tribal peoples in the vicinity. But on a nearby oil-and-gas pipeline project, the construction contractor decided not to hire and train tribal people for skilled jobs because this would have alienated them from their traditional economic activities. It depends on the project, the country, and the moment in history whether tribal people are excluded or included in such work. In Bastar their role was expected to be menial and marginal, but their compliance with the project was more or less presumed.

Forestry planners complain that tribal people are uneducated, ill-disciplined for industrial work, suspicious, unmotivated, and even lazy. In addition, governments discover that tribal people are susceptible to revolutionary organizations or objectives—nontribal and tribal people sometimes make common cause to restrict or delay tropical forestry. Such organized actions can exact a higher price for the commodity. More problematic than their poverty, tribal people's objectives seem obscure and unconnected with those of the consumer societies, the governments, and the corporations that want their trees. Tribal people appear to be satisfied with something other than industrial forest development. Planners debate what that might be, and whether the tribals' source of satisfaction is compatible with "the general good" or "the national interest"—code words for the objectives of the government. Finally, these inaccessible regions where forests and tribes lie are very often border regions between countries or between dominant ethnic groups. When conflict occurs, as in South America or Southeast Asia, the forests and tribes can become hostage to the conflict or can be destroyed in the process. The development of tribal people's economics within a national scheme thus becomes of greater significance to economic planners. But to social planners, the conservation of cultures and cultural diversity—such as languages, arts, technologies, tribal knowledge of the environment—is extremely important. Cultural diversity seems to be at least as important as diversity in trees or wildlife: these are interdependent in the tropical forests.

The wildlife problem is equally complex and is intimately related to the problem of tropical forests. Whether majestic or ordinary, many animal species inhabiting the tropical forest are endangered by its conversion. Without alternatives, they face stress or extinction. At the very least, stress will alter their patterns of reproduction. For tribal people, such changes will represent a loss of food or income sources and a loss of great meaning in their lives: the forest inhabitants are mainly hunters. Outsiders also hunt these animals as sources of food and aphrodisiacs, or to provide fur coats, hunting trophies, or animals for experiments. Such uses may compete with the uses of tribal people, although the scale of extraction differs in every place. Some tribal people also profit marginally from supplying these external needs. A relatively recent issue is the concept of animal rights. Animals themselves have, in the judgment of some people, a right to live undisturbed in their habitat and to endure as species. Advocates have been developing the politics necessary to assert these animal rights—"Is wildlife endangered in Bastar forests?" asked lobbyists in Washington, D.C., and in India. But the Bastar wildlife problem is apparently insoluble by legislation: the conflict of interests involves parties too far separated by geography and levels of power, linked by the media and the markets, but seldom by jurisdiction and enforcement.

The firewood problem—an old problem—became fashionable again in the 1970s. Poor people in and around forests (including tribals) need fuel for cooking and heating. They take firewood from the forest, as they always have. But now there is a greatly increased cut, as the poor in the city slums—who have no gas or electric connections—buy firewood for the same purposes. Firewood moves hundreds of miles, to markets insensitive to the rate of extraction. It competes there against such alternative sources as natural gas, coal, propane, electricity, dung, jute stalks, and solar power—each with separate environmental consequences. Forest districts in India have become deficient in firewood, and tribal people experience keen competition with their needs. Often branches of trees are taken, spoiling a tree's growth but leaving its trunk. As firewood gets scarce and the price goes up, the poor people in unforested areas suffer the most. Forestry planners have become nervous about trying to satisfy the firewood needs of urban populations. In countries like India, foresters have long been unsuccessful in creating adequate firewood plantations; but illegal cutting proceeds very rapidly where populations are large and needs are great.

The Bastar project deliberately addressed a specific aspect of the problem of tropical forests in India. Although nearly 23 percent of the land area was classified as forest, employment in this sector was provided for only 0.2 percent of the Indian labor force, according to the World Bank's project documents.[9] Whereas agriculture contributed about 45 percent of Gross Development Product (GDP), forestry contributed "a mere 1.3 percent of GDP," and its contribution to export and foreign exchange earnings was "insignificant," according to the World Bank. The forests of India, 97 percent owned by the state, were under pressure from use by the public despite legal attempts to protect them. In general their regeneration was slow and partial, but the "Dome area," including Bastar in central India, had a high volume of timber.

Such natural forests were inaccessible, and there was no available technology "to handle the wide range of presently unmarketable species" of which the forests were composed.

What is worse, said the World Bank, the market in India for forest products was undersupplied: consumption of paper was being limited by restriction on imports and decrease in domestic supply. Yet the demand for industrial wood was predicted (in 1971) to increase three-fold by 1990, a demand that could not be met without increasing forest productivity—that is, a large-scale program of fast-growing species. Such species were important, because even an immediate beginning of tropical pine plantations would not meet the predicted demand for long-fibered material in 1990. The technical problem was that results of the limited trials of these new species were insufficient to justify their being repeated on a large scale. Something had to be done, said the Bank's planners, because the present trends (if unchecked) would lead to "a continued depletion and degradation of the forests, which would be permanently lost." An incoherent forest industry would develop, trying to meet increasing demand, producing at relatively high costs, and using only part of the potential forest resources.

If such assumptions were correct, these trends could not go on indefinitely. Note that demand for industrial wood was highlighted—not for firewood, house-building materials, or fencing as removed by people in and around the forests. In fact, there were no reliable estimates of these other uses in India at the time. A wide range of species was presently of little market value, whether or not it played a crucial role in forest ecology. The processes by which degradation occurs were not discussed, nor was the interplay of uses and forest-users—cardboard boxes versus firewood. No analysis was made of the low contribution of forestry and logging either to employment or to GNP. It would be misleading, surely, if one concluded that the forests were economically unimportant. What may have been revealed here is that such statistics are unrealistic. Finally, there was no mention of the people who live in the forest.

As for the big picture, the World Bank warned of a balance of payments deficit of U.S. $2.4 billion for India in 1975–1976. India's cost of importing its fuel alone would increase sharply: in the previous year, cost of imports had increased 47 percent and, besides fuel, there were sharp needs to import food, fertilizer, "and other essentials." Food production the year before had dropped dramatically. Inflation was running at 30 percent annually. India had to earn more foreign exchange and spend less on imports, including paper. The fiscal situation was "seemingly out of hand." Half of the balance-of-payments deficit was being made up by foreign aid (see table 2); that is, about $1.3 billion in 1974–1975. Of that amount, aid from "Eastern Europe" came to about $100 million plus some barter agreements; the total dependence of India's development on OECD (Organization for Economic Cooperation and Development) country financing, the World Bank, and the International Monetary Fund (IMF) is thus clear. Half of the $2.4 billion deficit, the Bank noted, "can be covered from gross disbursements of

TABLE 2
India
External Finance, 1974–1975
(In thousand U.S. dollars)

1. Debt repayable in foreign currency	11,612,000
2. Debt repayable through export of goods	784,000
3. Total debt outstanding and disbursed	12,396,000
4. Debt service ratio	19.0%
5. Official aid disbursements	1,860,000
6. Official aid amortization (equivalent to debt service)	750,000
7. Transactions with IMF	515,000
8. IBRD loans outstanding and undisbursed	762,000
9. IDA loans outstanding and undisbursed	3,393,000
10. IFC investments	51,800
11. World Bank's share of India's outstanding public debt (1974)	23.0%
12. World Bank's portion of India's debt service payments, 1974–1975	14.0%

Currency 1975: U.S. $1 = Rupee 8.91 (official), Rupee 7.72 (spot rate); Rupee 1 = U.S. $0.112 (official), U.S. $0.129 (spot rate); Rs 1 million = U.S. $112,250.
Source: Selected from IBRD / IDA P–1733–IN, 1975.

previously committed foreign aid." In 1969–1970 the World Bank had provided 34 percent of India's external assistance. When the Bastar project began, this amount was over 42 percent. India was one among a number of countries in this predicament.

From this analysis of India's overall development problem, and the problem of forests and the forest industry, the Bank concluded that trials of fast-growing pine species, new technology, and studies of increased industrial forestry productivity "should be started immediately to help launch a sound forestry development policy." Thus it was that the Bastar Technical Assistance Project (TAP), using Caribbean pine (*Pinus caribaea*), was given a pioneer role by the World Bank in the modernization of India's forests and in the solution to the problem of tropical forestry. This was exactly how the new technology of man-made industrial forest plantations was being transferred to other countries. And, it was argued, the process should begin in India.

The application of apparently rapid solutions to issues of intractable difficulty characterizes the global process of social, political, and economic change. This process, whether it is regressive or progressive, whether it is growth or contraction, is labeled "development." In this process, the divergent interests of development planners in Washington, D.C., and of tribal people in Indian forests are joined. Our final purpose in this introduction is to set the Bastar project and the problems it addressed into the popular discourse about international development—in particular, the development of tribal people.

The term *development* comes from Latin—"to unwrap, to disentangle, to rid free": it has slowly acquired two connotations. The first conveys a gradual and natural progression from lower or simpler to higher or more complex states—something is fully developed when it reaches a state of vigorous life or action. The second suggests bringing something out or rendering it visible—developing a news story, or developing a chess piece to a position of greatest service in a player's game plan. A tension exists between these two connotations: the first implies the unfolding of a natural law, and the second indicates the actions of an intervening agency. The first suggests some self-determination; the second suggests some interference. People shift back and forth in their reliance on these two connotations: sometimes it is logical to speak of a natural unfolding; sometimes of an intervening agency. This is particularly true if one works for such an intervening agency as the World

Bank. The image of the relative helplessness of tribal people in India inspires thinking about an intervening agency which could accelerate gradual processes.

The process of international development must respond to the relentless pressures of competing interests. The state pursues its insatiable appetite for more revenue and thus for more control; the poor people maintain a continuous search for necessities (such as firewood) or for sources of minor benefits; the private sector and multilateral agencies continue to pursue new sources of profitability—no matter how distant or dubious—to adjust to the trend toward declining profitability and the potential exhaustion of current supplies. Expertise tends to assist the state and the private sector in the pursuit of their interests: in the Bastar case, there is little evidence supporting the interests of the poor people in the forest. The problems to which the Bastar project was addressed were not defined by people living in Bastar.

Each of these competing interests needs new technology and new techniques to assist it. Poor people need technology too. Technology transfer has thus been at the center of the international process because no one waits for indigenous evolution and everyone desires some form of acceleration—for different reasons. This holds true in agriculture, health, population, food processing, housing, and so on. In Bastar, the forests are diminishing through a number of causes. Natural forest regeneration takes eighty years, if it is undisturbed. During the next eighty years, competition among various interests in the Bastar forests will probably increase. Conflict will probably occur—perhaps, as elsewhere, becoming endemic. Disturbance of the forest's regenerative process appears inevitable, so full replacement of the forests within eighty years seems unlikely.

Technology transfer was also at the center of the Bastar project: in fact, all the problems of tropical forestry, of tribal people, of wildlife, and of firewood seemed to be resolved by the idea of man-made industrial tree plantations. Plantations are an old form of organization in India: the first teak plantation was established in the seventeenth century for the navy of the Marathas; the first gmelina plantation, in 1930. But here was a fresh approach; here was an internationally accepted idea using an existing species ready to grow in fifteen to thirty years on a very large scale. No genetic adaptation seemed to be required. In fact, the Caribbean pine had already been on trial in Bastar for many years. A brand-new corporation, proposed in an earlier government commission's report, would be completely in charge. The whole package—the technique—seemed timely and appropriate.

The international development community, in which the World Bank and the Government of India are key players, is not just a faceless collection of divergent interests. It is also people alive to ideas, which have their own politics and fashions. If the industrial plantation technique could "somehow" be balanced with the social forestry technique, then other developments could occur which would make Bastar "the Ruhr of the East." All this expectation was largely on the side of the second connotation of the term "development"—that it signifies the activities of external agencies more than an unfolding of properties inherent within a situation like Bastar. Some foresters said that, if left alone, the tribals would virtually destroy the forest. All outsiders drew the conclusion that nothing of economic and social significance would happen in Bastar unless outsiders engineered and achieved it. That, they said, is development. But what about the problem of tribal people's development?

There is a tradition in India, traceable to the preachings of Mahatma Gandhi, to the British Utilitarians, and perhaps back to Victorian moralism, of perceiving development, be it of tribal or low-caste people, as "uplift." Remaining in common parlance today, the notion of uplift implies more than economic improvement: it is an all-encompassing concept, with connotations of social, cultural, and moral transformation. The end result of uplift—"the upliftment of the downtrodden" is the usual slogan—projects a benevolent sociocultural integration with an essentially Hindu mainstream life-style, and the achievement of economic parity within that life-style.

Tribal uplift, then, shares with the concept of development the implication of change involving new objectives, ideas, methods, and forms of relationships while, in a global sense, emphasizing for tribal people a moral order with some approximation to Hindu orthodoxy. Tribal uplift also shares with development the modus operandi of imposition, even where the philosophy is one of consultation. It is a fact, for anyone studying development from the point of view of the people being "developed," that almost all plans and projects are imposed. The Bastar project was no exception, even when it was (vaguely) stated that the tribals would be involved.

Although tribal development and uplift are relatively modern concepts, the fact of imposition has an ancient background in India. Considered to be the aboriginal inhabitants of India, tribal people first experienced outside imposition some 3,000 years ago when the so-called Aryans swept down from the Central Asian steppes. Successive waves of these invaders, with their superior military technology, eventually displaced the aboriginals from the northern plains of India. This set a pattern that recurred periodically over the millennia whenever and wherever there was continued tribal-outsider interaction: after the initial countless battles, extended contact with foreign peoples was usually avoided as the tribal groups retreated into more inaccessible, often more hilly and inhospitable regions—like Bastar. Where repeated contact and retreat left the aboriginals nowhere farther to go—in other words, where their lands were alienated, their livelihoods undermined, and their identities threatened—relations with the outsiders became so completely unsatisfactory that open rebellion and violence were the only remaining channels of self-expression. In some cases, where tribals were structurally and numerically weak, absorption into the developing caste system of the invaders took place. Where the tribals had nothing worthwhile to expropriate—for example, in the case of very remote hunting and gathering groups—they were left to themselves after brief encounters. There were also some groups (in India's northeast) for whom contact was very late, where retreat did not take place, but where resistance to political control was great. Thus, among the tribes of northeastern India (in particular the Nagas), Christianity was accepted from European missionaries, but the later force of Indian nationalism was, and to some extent still is, actively resisted. In some cases, tribal people's resistance has been met with government military force, again and again.

The British colonial entrapment and partial unification of India's diverse cultures and kingdoms—in a colonially typical, retrogressive fashion—began the process of tribal development. It was the "unification" by the British, and some of their methods of accomplishing it, which saw a proliferation of tribal movements and which repeated the pattern of contact, retreat, and rebellion. Several millenarian movements, as well, had their origins in the gradual British annexation of Indian territories.

Aggrievance over the long list of oppression, injustice, and exploitation, or, conversely, the view that sees only the benefits resulting from British administration, and the detailed evidence documenting these divergent perceptions, need not detain us here.[10] Nonetheless, two general facts should be noted. First, the British, in their extension of interest into peripheral tribal areas, opened the way for commercially oriented agents and land-hungry immigrants to penetrate and take economic advantage of so-called unsophisticated peoples. Second, British land settlements turned commonly held tribal land into individual private properties that could be bought and sold—and ruinously taxed. The results of these two facts are unequivocally presented in this general picture:

> During and since British rule, there has been increasing encroachment on tribal hill territories and oppression of tribespeople by European and Indian planters, by government usurpation of forest areas, by landlords, merchants, and moneylenders from the plains and by government officials. To the loss of large tribal areas was added exploitation in such forms as rack-renting, unequal terms of trade, usury, corvee and even slave labour and the obligation to grow cash crops for little or no return.[11]

It is in view of these conditions that tribal insurrection and violent resistance can be understood.

This is not to say that it was not also (belatedly) understood by some British officials, who finally began to address "the tribal situation" by setting up ameliorative measures. These measures, however, were only in small part effective, because legislation cordoning off tribal areas in remote parts of India in order to eliminate the depredations of outsiders largely failed in light of continued exploitation.

Such legislation during the last years of British control in India did, nevertheless, touch off a vociferous controversy over the initial policies on the subject of the aboriginal tribes. Although some anthropologically minded administrators advocated "a policy of protection, which in specific cases involved even a measure of seclusion, Indian politicians attacked the idea of segregation and seclusion on the grounds that it threatened to deepen and perpetuate divisions within the Indian nation, and delayed the aboriginals' integration into the rest of the population." [12] Emerging from this controversy, various proposals were put forward under the headings of gradual, controlled acculturation; integration while preserving acceptable cultural features (art, music, dance, etc.); and complete assimilation into the Hindu socio-cultural mainstream. Inheriting this unresolved controversy at independence, the new Indian government adopted the integrationist approach, beginning its own development policies with a set of protective constitutional provisions under the "scheduled tribes" legislation (a list or "schedule" of groups guaranteed certain benefits, such as reservation of jobs for tribals in government service, seats for them in legislatures, and availability of special funds for development programs in tribal areas).

The problem of tribal development as seen by the Indian government is thus one of bringing about the economic advancement of tribal societies without at the same time destroying their traditional cultures. The planning and implementation of this development policy in the first decades of independence has proved less than successful. For instance:

> The Government's insistence on the fulfillment of specific physical targets laid down by planners without any knowledge of local conditions led to the expenditure of funds on projects of little utility . . . houses were built only to be washed away in the rainy season, basketry centres started where there are no bamboos, and bee-keeping established where there are no flowers. [13]

The little interest tribal people had shown for such central government development programs was consequently lost. These failures of implementation, while contributing to tribal mistrust (as well as creating an understandable apathy) toward centralist schemes, were relatively innocuous—relative, that is, to the devastation originating with state government responses to the problem of tribal development.

One of the worst cases, thoroughly documented over a period of thirty years, involved the neighboring state of Andhra Pradesh in southern India.[14] There, in the years following independence, corrupt forest and revenue officers actively assisted settlers from other parts of India to seize tribal lands. The same officers, with few exceptions, were easily bribed to falsify land registration documents; would use force, if needed, to remove tribals from their traditional farmlands; would regularly prohibit tribals from collecting forest produce; and would allow nontribals, for a fee, to cut down entire forests, altering the ecological balance forever. In Andhra Pradesh, legislative protection and benevolent tribal development policies were virtually ignored.

Instead, the state government actively engaged, even prior to 1947, "in creating a new class of wandering, landless, uneducated and hopeless tribes people. . . . It is little wonder that there have been several revolts against the mistrusted government among tribal peoples, or that some of them have seen the revolutionary Naxalite movement as their best hope."[15] Andhra Pradesh, it will be noted, is not the only state which so offends.

But what of the central government's professed commitment to benevolent tribal development? How is it that so much of the tribal development effort results in so little? Is it possible, in fact, to answer these questions without taking into consideration the international forces of development? The answer to this last question is readily given: no.

It has become almost axiomatic that the "rapid incorporation of virtually every part of the world into the international political and economic 'community' marks the end, or the beginning of the end, for isolated and exotic tribal communities and also for complex and archaic civilizations. In this sense, and only in this sense, the unification of the world is nearly complete."[16] The process of the Bastar project is being repeated in the uranium mines of the Australian outback, the forests of Brazil, the oil fields of Canada, and the steppes of the USSR. The "unification of the world" and the end of tribal communities are not simply matters of modern technology or postindustrial transformation. The process is a highly sensitive one, involving definitions of the rights and needs of aboriginal peoples, the politics of nationalism, and the imperatives faced by all countries in their continuing quest for economic prosperity. The interplay of all these factors can and does create conditions of hierarchy which commit certain groups of people to the likelihood of extreme suffering and degradation.

But another possibility does exist: the development of resources need not sacrifice tribal interests. It is possible to communicate the human ecological considerations intrinsic to economic change. To explore this possibility, to document and analyze its aspects within a particular context, and to suggest approaches toward achieving a balance of local and national developmental interests, are the primary reasons for presenting the following account of the Bastar Technical Assistance Project in the context of the whole economic and political development of the district.

CHAPTER 2

The Tribals and Their Kingdom

We do not mind the fine so much as we mind the contempt of the government for our tradition. —Tribal Headman, Bastar, 1978

THE MODERN district of Bastar lies in the southeast corner of Madhya Pradesh state in central India. With an area of 39,060 square kilometers, it is the largest district in India, nearly the size of Belgium. Census figures of 1981 show the population of Bastar to be 1,840,499, of which close to 70 percent is classified as scheduled tribes.[1] Population density at 47/km^2 is well below the Indian average, although this is up from 39/km^2 in 1971. Nonetheless, Bastar is a relatively underpopulated area, and this fact has encouraged, over a lengthy span of time, considerable in-migration, mainly from areas to the north where Hindi or Hindi dialect is spoken. In more recent times, this fact has undoubtedly played a major role in the decision by the Government of India to try to resettle large numbers of refugees from erstwhile East Pakistan, now Bangladesh. Of the total population, 98 percent is rural.

Topographically, the greater part of the district is an undulating plateau of about 650 meters which drops to near sea level on the plains of southwest Bastar. There are a few hilly ranges in the south and west, with peaks rising to 1,300 meters. Bastar is bisected by the Indravati River, which provides the district with north and south designations. Two other important rivers drain the region: the Mahanadi in the north, flowing to the Bay of Bengal, and the Sabari River running south into the Godavari River of Andhra Pradesh. The perennially flowing Indravati originates in the hills of Orissa, neighboring to the east, and flows across Bastar's western boundary into Chanda district of Maharashtra state.

A large part of Bastar (56.8 percent) is covered by tropical, moist,

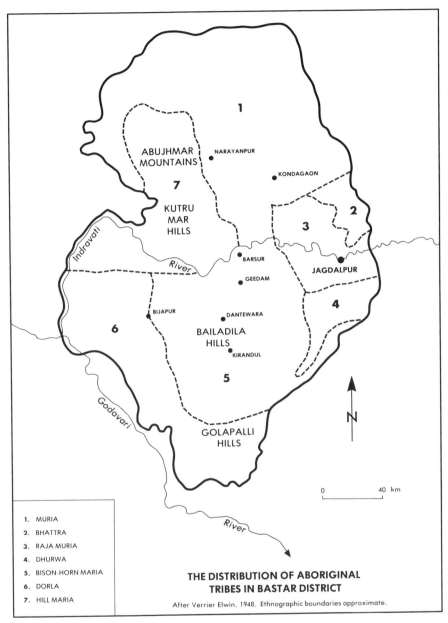

1. MURIA
2. BHATTRA
3. RAJA MURIA
4. DHURWA
5. BISON-HORN MARIA
6. DORLA
7. HILL MARIA

**THE DISTRIBUTION OF ABORIGINAL
TRIBES IN BASTAR DISTRICT**

After Verrier Elwin, 1948. Ethnographic boundaries approximate.

Still an ethnological enigma unlikely to be fully explicated, the origin of Bastar's tribal populations is speculated to lie in South India. Known to themselves as Koitor and to outsiders as Gonds, whose numerical strength and historic importance are unrivaled in India, most Bastar tribals speak Dravidian-based dialects. Latest census figures for Bastar show a population of 1,840,499 of which 98% is rural and 70% tribal. Density at 47/km² is well below the Indian average though up from 39/km² in 1971. Thus relatively under-populated, Bastar has attracted considerable, largely unwanted, in-migration since at least the 1800s from Hindi- and Hindi-dialect-speaking areas to the north.

deciduous forests. These include about 100 species, mostly such hard-woods as teak, sal (*Shorea robusta*), and laurel. The balance, about 20 percent, is made up of bamboo.[2] For India, this is an unusually dense forest cover. State and central government authorities view these forests as a highly valuable commercial resource. Bastar's other major resource lies in mineral deposits, especially the rich iron ore areas of Raoghat in north Bastar and of Bailadila in the south. The Bailadila deposits have been developed and the extracted ore is sent to Japan on long-term contract. For this purpose, Bastar's only rail line has been constructed to connect the mines with the port of Visakapatnam in Andhra Pradesh.

This rail line and a meager network of roads serve to indicate a general poverty of transportational and communicational facilities. These find their nexus in the capital of Jagdalpur, a town of some 35,000 inhabitants. (Predominantly, these latter are immigrants from north India, although they include a substantial number of Oriya-speaking Brahmans.) In addition to the few paved roads, a number of fair-weather forest tracks lead through various portions of the interior of Bastar, but these tend to skirt most areas without penetrating them. This scant network of transportation arteries, except for the Jagdalpur route, is plied by a rather infrequent bus service. Otherwise, "the principal means of locomotion [is] travel by foot over jungle paths."[3] For this logistical reason, there is relatively little administrative intervention in tribal affairs. It is revealing to note that most tribal village settlement patterns avoid proximity to the main roads.

For purposes of administration, Bastar is divided into eight district subdivisions, or *tehsils*: Bhanupratapur, Kanker, Narayanpur, and Kondagaon in the north; Bijapur, Dantewara, and Konta in the south; and Jagdalpur tehsil straddling the central, eastern section of the district. The tehsil headquarters, for which the tehsils are named and where revenue and judicial functions are concentrated, are situated in relation to the distribution of population. At the apex of the administrative hierarchy, located in Jagdalpur, is the Collector, an official who directs and oversees all judicial, revenue and developmental activities in the Bastar district. The district bureaucracy is in large part patterned on the British system of administration of pre-independence India. With minor variations, this system is still cumbersomely prevalent over most of the country.

Although a civil servant, the Collector has in many respects the most powerful political position in the region. When the Bastar project began in 1976, planners and tribals faced a situation in which the Collector was in fact sharing power with the Forest Department in more than half of the district territory. The Forest Department operated in administrative "ranges," "circles," and "catchments," which were not contiguous with the Collector's tehsils; in the reserve and protected forest the department's judgment was generally more influential than that of any civil administrators. At times, elements of both systems were in disagreement. In its style, the Forest Department operated like a paramilitary organization, with policing and some judicial powers. Its control over the purchase of forest products from tribals (due to forest nationalization) as well as resale outside the district gave the department influence beyond the boundaries of its demarcated territories. The Collector would thus need sometimes to balance the interests of one department against those of another. Not all Collectors have been enthusiastic about the development of industrial forestry in Bastar. Some administrators, before and after Bastar's integration with India in 1947, have supported tribals in confrontations with elements of the state apparatus.

The tribal people of Bastar are generically known as *Gonds*, a term perceived as pejorative by many of those to whom it is applied. While it would thus be preferable to use their own name for themselves (*Koitor*), the terms *Gond* and *Gondi* (denoting the Dravidian, unwritten language spoken by Gonds) are retained for reasons of their pervasiveness and antiquity in the anthropological and historical literature. This literature reveals that the Gonds of Bastar are only a few of the many Gond groups that populate the area covered by the present state of Madhya Pradesh.[4] Gond groups are also in eastern Maharashtra and northern Andhra Pradesh, and some minor branches are in Orissa. Their total population is over four million, out of an all-India tribal population that has probably surpassed forty million.[5] This, along with a political prominence reaching back several centuries, supports the assertion that "among the tribal populations of India there is none which rivals [the Gonds] in numerical strength and historic importance."[6] Strictly speaking, however, it is doubtful whether any such group exists. Rather than possessing any apparent cultural or linguistic homogeneity, fewer than 50 percent of the so-called Gonds speak Gondi; of those who do, many speak dialects that are barely, if at all, intelligible to one another. To this diversity must be added a variety of types of subsistence activities, ranging from the shifting axe-and-hoe cultivation of isolated hill people to the sedentary plough agriculture of rice-growing plains groups, who are barely distinguishable in most respects from their Hindu neighbors.

Ethnographically, Bastar is representative of this diversity. Taken together, the "tribes" of Bastar—the number ranging upward from seven, depending on which specifications are used—can roughly be assigned a position on a scale bounded by criteria of "least Hinduized" to "most Hinduized." Of the three main groups, the *Hill Maria* would clearly be among the least Hinduized; the *Muria* and *Bison-horn Maria* would be situated around the middle; and such groups as the *Bhattra, Halba, Dhurwa,* and *Dorla* would come closest to the Hindu end of the scale. This does not imply that fixed and definite boundaries are associated with these groups. Ambiguity, and a corresponding proba- bility of status competition, most surrounds the Muria title, which primarily denotes the tribal people of Narayanpur and Kondagaon tehsils. But it also refers to, and is used by, the very Hinduized tribals living in the Jagdalpur area. For example, a Bison-horn Maria living in Dantewara tehsil but close to the Jagdalpur border may deny his appellation and say instead that he is a Muria; a Jagdalpur Muria may further distinguish himself by saying he is a Raja Muria, a Muria having been in close association with the former kings of Bastar. The Raja Muria, in turn, may call himself a Bhattra, in an attempt at self- promotion, while the Bhattras, and here we reach the most-Hinduized extreme, subdivide into higher and lower categories, both of which are more caste-like than tribal.[7]

In this connection, mention should be made of the "purely" Hindu castes of Bastar, which include the Brahman, *Dakar* (warrior-cultivator), *Kallar* and *Sundi* (distiller), *Rawat* (cowherd), Muslim and Christian (*Isai*), *Mahar* and *Ganda* (weaver), *Ghasia* (ornament-maker), *Lohar* (blacksmith), and *Chamar* (leather-worker). A distinction must be drawn between those Hindu castes that have immigrated to Bastar—for example, the Oriya Brahmans and various *Bania* (merchant) castes from Maharashtra, northern Madhya Pradesh and Uttar Pradesh who are settled in Jagdalpur and other semiurban areas—and Hindu castes that are indigenous, in a sense, "homegrown." Excluding Brahmans, who have always been imported in some fashion or other, most of these castes have been made up of tribal people who have taken to Hindu occupations, but who have not lost their tribal sociocultural integrity except for a minimal measure of ritual exclusion from tribal life. The point here is that, while the idiom of caste has penetrated tribal society right up to the foothills of the Abujhmar (the remotest corner of Bastar), the ideological or sociological substance of caste—concepts of purity and pollution, the complementary separation of status and authority, in other words, a rigorous structure of hierarchy—is largely undetectable beyond the confines of immigrant Hindu population centers.

The social organization of the Bastar Gonds is based on patrilineal clan exogamy, all clans being either *akomama* or *dadabayi* to one another—that is either "wife-clan" or "brother-clan." The system becomes something of a moiety with patrilocal, cross-cousin marriage. Clan structure is typically segmentary, with old clans splitting up into new clans under the pressure of population growth, or, in some cases, becoming extinct due to administrative, political, or biological disruptions.

Spatial organization of social groups follows basically two patterns: Hill Maria clans tend to predominate, each to an entire village, with a group of agnatically related clan-villages forming a "territorial brotherhood"; much more densely populated, Bison-horn Maria and Muria areas contain non-nucleated villages with plural clan residence, although all are bounded (at least conceptually) within territorial brotherhoods linked to a founding clan.[8] This complexity defies the simplistic belief among planners that "the tribals" are one coherent group with a uniform relation to the forest which can easily be managed by the state. Actually, industrial development would affect differently each tribal group of Bastar, according to its degree of economic dependence on the resources to be expropriated. For example, with the nearly total economic dependence of the Hill Marias of Abujhmar, the impact on them of industrial forestry would obviously be greater than on the settled agriculturalists around Jagdalpur. Nevertheless, the forest (where it still exists) has been a source of provision and livelihood for nearly all Bastar's inhabitants.

Bastar tribal society is at one with Bastar tribal religion, for the differentiation of clan is identical with the differentiation of deity. Clans are both unified and separated by clan deities (more broadly, "ancestral deities"), displaying a continuum of conception and conceptual transformation culminating in the all-inclusiveness of the Earth—specifically, the Earth Goddess *Tallur Mutte* among the Muria, *Tallin Ochur* among the Bison-horn Maria, and *Talo Dai* among the Hill Maria. These are only the more generic names among many for the supreme female deity. Many further "refractions" occur in localized contexts, such as the "Village Mother." As posited by Grigson, "the fundamental relation between the Earth, the clan-god and the Village Mother . . . is that the clan-god is the Earth in its dealings with the clan, and the Mother the Earth in its dealings with the village."[9] As part of these relations of equivalence, brought into relation by the same transformational process, are the Hindu tutelary goddess *Danteshwari* (equivalent to Tallur Mutte, etc.), and, until quite recently, the Bastar kings, who were credited with divine status.

In terms of tribal economy, all the Gonds of Bastar have a tradition of swidden agriculture; the Hill Maria still practice it almost exclusively, while the Muria and Bison-horn Maria, even though strongly attached to their "slash-and-burn" preferences, have taken to nonshifting rice cultivation as their predominant mode of food production.[10] In addition, the Gonds supplement their economic activities with wage labor and the collection of minor forest produce. Although not rigorously determined, "the relative contribution of each sector to the economy is approximately as follows: agriculture 40–45 percent; minor forest produce 15–25 percent; and wage labor 30–35 percent."[11] It is important to note, however, that the collection of forest produce has likely been underestimated, and that all Bastar tribals rely more heavily than indicated on forest foraging to supplement food supplies (especially in lean monsoon periods), for construction and fuel sources, and for minor commercial exploitation.

The Indian governmental consensus on Bastar's economic character is that it is a "backward," "depressed" area, suffering from "scant diversification of the economy and . . . poor industrialisation."[12] To government planners, these indications of economic backwardness are conceived along with the existing, relatively abundant timber and mineral resources of the district, leading to the promotion of Bastar as the potential "El Dorado of modern times . . . the Ruhr of [the] East."[13] Similar, if less flamboyant, prognostications date back to the 1850s and 1860s, when Bastar, as a semi-independent kingdom, came under the sway of British suzerainty. All such views included the perception of tribal people as a burdensome problem in the push for economic development. In the extreme case, Bastar's resource potential is discussed as if its tribal majority did not even exist.[14] In the most common conception, however, be it Noble Savage or squalid degenerate, the caricatures of tribal people with their alleged lazy and orgiastic lifestyles continue to be taken as firm realities and obstacles to be overcome in the desire to develop Bastar's more or less unexploited resource base.

Now we shall look to the historical background of Bastar in order accurately to place the tribal population in relation to its natural and human (i.e., nontribal) environment. These relations are the context of contemporary socioeconomic developments, in particular of the Bastar forestry project.

Bastar is not unique in India for having been a Hindu kingdom with a predominantly non-Hindu tribal populace. There were similar kingdoms in what are now Orissa to the east and Maharashtra to the west, as well as to the north, in what were called the Chattisgarh feudatory states. It is also not unique that the monarchs of Bastar were firmly believed to be divine kings who, as such, exerted a complete spiritual and temporal hegemony over their subjects. The economic foundation of this hegemony, in Bastar as well as in many of the other princely states in central India, was characterized by an interdependence of king and court with tribal followers which allowed for flexibility to the extent of noninterference in regard to tribal customary practices. Such practices included a strong, religiously sanctioned commitment to swidden cultivation and an equally firm dependence on hunting and gathering of forest vegetation. Especially in the lean monsoon months, the forest guaranteed the otherwise precarious survival of many of the tribal people of states like Bastar. As mentioned above, this last characteristic remains an important source of tribal incomes and sustenance.

The particularities of Bastar are, of course, another matter. Size alone distinguishes the area as the largest Hindu-tribal kingdom to have persisted into the twentieth century. Its isolation, its remoteness and difficulty of access, and its insalubrious malarial conditions have all contributed to Bastar's reputation as an unparalleled backwater of Indian history and geography. Owing to the British expansionist push for increased revenue-producing territory in the mid-1800s, however, a certain amount of official interest was generated in the inhabitants of Bastar. This mainly fiscal curiosity led British officialdom to send some of its more intrepid agents to explore the area. The information thus provided was intended to improve upon previous reports that for the most part Bastar consisted of "naked savages living on roots and sprigs, and hunting for strangers to sacrifice."[15]

Unhappily for the British, these agents were unable to present much ground for commercial optimism. The official definition of the problem was, and remains for the present Indian government, one of "savagery" versus "civilization." Glasfurd's 1862 report, laying the lines for future policy, concludes with these remarks:

> The country, it will be perceived, is an interminable forest, with the exception of a small cultivated tract around Jagdalpur, intersected by high mountain ranges, which present serious obstacles to traffic. . . . The inhabitants are composed of rude, uncivilized tribes of Gonds, in some parts almost savages, who shun contact with strangers, and have but few wants which they cannot supply themselves; honest and interesting to the Ethnologist perhaps but a race who prefer the solitude of forests to the bustle of towns, and the freedom of the savage to all the allurements and comforts of civilization. With such a country and such inhabitants, rapid progress and improvement cannot be looked for; and any efforts to open out the Dependency, with the hope of immediately stimulating trade, or rather creating it where it never existed, would end in disappointment. Our efforts for the present should be to open up a few important lines on which traffic already exists, and to ameliorate the conditions of the people by the introduction of a better system of criminal and judicial procedure than at present is in force at Jagdalpur. . . . The fact is that the Dependency must be civilized.[16]

Glasfurd, his superiors and policy makers, and most of the local officials sent out to implement the opening up and civilizing of Bastar, did not see or understand that there must have been, and still were, "institutions or systems in this apparently unordered Bastar to have kept her together and free" from outside interference for the four centuries prior to the advent of the British.[17] And this special system constituted the uniqueness of Bastar: an egalitarian tribal society smoothly integrated with a hierarchical Hindu polity.

Although there is evidence of a Hindu presence (in the form of temple ruins and inscriptions dating back to the ninth century), it was not until approximately the year 1450 that the Bastar kingdom became a recognizable entity. This came about upon the flight into the Bastar area of one of the most ancient royal dynasties of southern India, the

Kakatiyas of Warangal. Fleeing from the invading armies of the southward expanding Mughul empire, the Kakatiyas took refuge in Bastar and set themselves to the task of establishing a kingdom in the jungle. While scant data are available to describe this process, it can be summarized as follows: subsequent to making a series of minor local conquests, a relatively small company of military retainers—headed by a fugitive Hindu prince and his close family—initiated a process of monarchical development. Faced with the problem of incorporating tribal societies under centralized, hierarchic authority, the Kakatiyas adopted (from already established Hindu-tribal kingdoms to the north) the solution of *weak* central authority structurally congruent with tribal polity. One can infer that the resulting monarchy was far from an exalted one. Remarks in British reports (e.g., Temple, 1862) indicate that the royal living conditions were little different—a slightly larger thatched hut—from those in their tribal surroundings. [18]

The next stage of political development saw the Kakatiyas establishing themselves at a center, beginning the process of moving to the more classical model of Hindu kingship. Still not on a large scale, a Hinduized domain began to be created, partially through the importation of Orissan Brahmans (and other service castes) and their subsequent influence on surrounding tribals.

The last political step in this direction was to construct a network of caste headmen for the Hinduized domain, the *khalsa*. Indirectly, this caused an adjustment in authority relations in the non-Hinduized, tribal areas. Concurrently, a royal bureaucracy took shape which was interposed between the court and village mainly for purposes of revenue collection. In the khalsa, however, it also exercised civil and criminal powers. The result of these political developments was that the kingdom of Bastar came to be implicitly divided into two parts. By this is meant not simply the khalsa and nonkhalsa, for the *zamindaris* (tributary minor Hindu chiefships) were also divided into a Hindu center and an outer, tribal part. Thus, one part took on an increasingly Hindu character with close connections to the state, while the other remained distinctly tribal, and in political and economic terms, experienced comparatively little intervention in customary practices.

Such, then, was the integrative nature of the relationship cultivated by the Kakatiyas with their Gond subjects. On a symbolic and ceremonial level, in terms of a certain sharing of rituals and ideology—most significantly, the divinity of the king—monarchy and tribal culture were tightly fused. On a practical level, so to describe economic relationships, interaction mainly consisted in periodic tribute payments, usually grain, and in relatively minor contributions of labor. Receiving in return the highly valued benedictions of protection and prosperity from their god-kings, the tribals were entitled as well to royal arbitration. Resolution of internal conflicts and socioeconomic problems took place at the annual royal *darbar*, or court, where the tribal groups could present their grievances and also their requests for royal patronage.

These essentially symbiotic relationships were conversely complemented by a high degree of independence. Aside from the occasional visitations of representatives from the loosely structured royal revenue administration, tribal socioeconomic organization was autonomous. The resources available to tribal society, the land and forest in which the tribals had customary though unwritten rights, were left to be managed without interference from Hindu overlordships. In turn, as a self-supporting system (albeit, more or less subsistential and located in an extremely difficult terrain), the Bastar monarchy could exist free of significant influence or interference from larger, more powerful forces beyond its borders. Such was, at least, the case from 1450 until the imposition of British suzerainty in 1853.

The British policy of "noninterference" in the affairs of the "Native States"—and it should be noted that such areas comprised two-fifths of India right up until 1948— gradually underwent a number of changes during the first half of the nineteenth century. From a position of virtually ignoring the inner workings of most states, to a disposition to draw up a great number of commercial treaties—later versions of which enjoined a more "civilized" mode of government—British policy by the 1850s developed a striking predilection for annexation. The motives for these changes were mixed. On one side were the "imperial interests of a trading company anxious to respond and rule cheaply." On the other side was the utilitarian zeal, often spurred by British missionaries crying out against oppression, which demanded administrative reform.[19] As Sir Richard Temple, the chief commissioner for Nagpur, concluded, "It is indeed most desirable that the [Bastar] Raja should learn to exercise his authority according to civilized ideas, and by noninterference should be made his own responsibility . . . on the wise management of the [Bastar State] . . . the gradual peopling of rich but scarcely inhabited tracts, and the civilizing of semi-barbarious tribes, will materially depend."[20] Thus intent on their civilizing mission, as well as on attempting to ensure the proper conditions for economic exploitation, the British began to pay increasingly closer attention to Bastar.

The transition from focusing that attention indirectly through the Maratha Nagpur state to dealing with Bastar as its paramount sovereign was effected by the British in 1853 through the annexation of the Nagpur state. Bastar then automatically became a tributary of the Government of India and entered into direct political relations with it. As more had become known of them, both Nagpur, with its areas of rich, black, cotton-producing soil, and Bastar as its subsidiary state with valuable timber reserves, had come to be seen as worthy additions to the list of subordinate allies of the British Empire. A more direct influence on administration and revenue extraction, one of course serving the other, was therefore justified in British policy. The British were thus preparing for the possibility of a direct takeover of the Bastar state. They were also preparing the way for the development of commercial interests in Bastar's forest resources.

CHAPTER 3

Forest-Tribe Relations

Reality would dictate that we should become more pragmatic and realistic in our approach and tailor policies that serve the interests of the nation, the forests and the tribals simultaneously. —Chief Secretary, Government of Madhya Pradesh, 1976

FROM the turn of the century, the conceptualization and organization of Bastar's resource base began to undergo gradual but definite transformations. On the pretext of royal succession problems, including self-destructive palace intrigues, the British took over longer and longer periods of direct administrative control. Of all the changes in administrative policy, the greatest impact resulted from new forest regulations. In the title of this chapter, the hidden term is *government*.

The magnitude of this impact can be gauged in light of a somewhat closer look at the traditional tribal relationships with the forest. In a poetic yet accurate manner, the following account depicts the tribal forest ecology:

> To a vast number of the tribal people the forest is their well-loved home, their livelihood, their very existence. It gives them food—fruits of all kinds, edible leaves, honey, nourishing roots, wild game and fish. It provides them with material to build their homes and practise their arts. By exploiting its produce they can supplement their meagre incomes. It keeps them warm with its fuel and cool with its grateful shade. Their religion leads them to [make] . . . special sacrifices to the forest gods; in many places offerings are made to a tree before it is cut and there are usually ceremonies before and after hunting . . . it is striking to see how in many of the myths and legends the deep sense of identity with the forest is emphasized. From time immemorial . . . the tribal people enjoyed the freedom to use the forest and hunt its animals and this has given them a conviction, which remains even today in their hearts that the forest belongs to them.[1]

The new forest regulations, embodied in the British policy formally initiated in 1894, negated the tribal conviction that the forest belonged to them. Instead, it asserted that the tribals had only certain rights and privileges in the forest, and that even these had to be restricted in favor of the "public benefit." In accordance with this policy, the forests were divided into three broad categories; namely, reserved forests, protected forests, and village forests. Reserved forests were exclusively for the use of the Forest Department except for certain minor concessions, such as gathering of the fruit of the trees and cutting of the grass, on payment of small dues.[2] In the reserved forests, the surrounding villagers had no rights other than the ones explicitly permitted by the state. The protected forests were also managed by the Forest Department, but the people of the surrounding villages had certain rights in them, such as gathering fruits and other produce of the trees, and cutting timber and wood specifically for the use of the villagers (but not for sale). They also had freedom to graze their livestock and hunt wild game for domestic purposes. Over the protected forests the villagers had all rights not specifically taken away by the state. The village forests were the communal property of the villagers. Since no regulatory authority was set out for this village common land, including forests on the land, the village forests tended to be successively depleted in most districts, as in Bastar. Even as grazing grounds, village commons were inefficiently managed and were quickly proven insufficient for the continuous influx of migrants and increase of population. These regulations, established at the end of the nineteenth century, prevailed beyond the 1927 amendments to the Forest Act and into the contemporary period. Taken together, all the rights of the tribal people in the forest were called *nistari*, which means to be free of (in this case tax). In theory the Forest Policy of 1894 clearly indicated that the state forests were to be managed in the interests of the people of India as a whole. But in practical terms, forest administration was almost exclusively intended for the purposes of ensuring revenue production for the state, even if the policy promoted a conservationist objective.

It would be more accurate to say that forest administration was part of the large-scale colonial enterprise in which the princely states, such as Bastar, were regarded as useful props of the empire. This was at the beginning of Kipling's day, when the princely (or native) states (there were 600 large and small states) were the "dark places of the earth." Relations were established expressing that "darkness" as a negative example for the populations of British India—dark places their work should "outshine." As the governor-general Lord Elphinstone put it:

> It appears to me to be in our interest as well as duty to use every means to preserve the allied Governments [princely states]. Their territories afford refuge to all those whose *habits of war*, intrigue or degradation make them incapable of remaining quiet in ours; and the contrast of their Government has a favourable effect on our subjects, who, while they feel the evils they are actually exposed to, are apt to forget the greater ones from which they have been delivered [emphasis added].[3]

It should be pointed out that the tribal (or Gond) "habits of war" are placed in their proper context in the following selection from an 1812 report on East India affairs. The report refers, among others, to the tribals of Bastar:

> The people in general although rude and barbarious, may yet be denominated warlike, as they have always distinguished themselves as bold and persevering champions of the great law of nature. Being driven to their wild unwholesome fastnesses among the mountains, they frequently descend in harvest time into the lowlands, to dispute the produce of their ancient rightful inheritance with the present possessions, but their incursions are desultory and singularly impelled by the pressing want of subsistence. [4]

It is also true that throughout Bastar history, and even into the contemporary period, it has been the potential "want of subsistence," or, to put it less euphemistically, the fear of starvation, that has been fundamental in any warlike behavior by the Gonds. This fear of famine contributed to their increasingly negative attitude toward the forestry project. This is characteristic of the absolute insecurity of subsistence economies.

In Bastar the measures taken to implement this forest administration, at first mostly conservational, and also the way in which they were implemented, were the principal causes of a widespread tribal rebellion in 1910. It is likely relevant to the complex chain of events leading to the 1910 rebellion that, just a year prior, "the first commercial exploitation started with a forest lease given to Mr. Becket and Co. for extraction of 25,000 railway sleepers from *sal* trees."[5] This gave impetus to active forest management, hitherto limited mainly to survey and demarcation work. Just before the rebellion, the notorious "forest villages" had been forcibly created as labor camps for captive workers whose first obligation was to the Forest Department. Some other tribal settlements in the forests were destroyed. In a report on the rebellion to the Foreign Department secretary, the government was informed of the main grievances of the tribals: the inclusion of village lands in reserves of forest, with a subsequent forced removal of villagers and the burning down of their dwellings; and, in general, the "high-handed treatment and unjust exactions on the part of Forest Officials."[6] The report admitted that these and numerous other grievances were largely genuine. In the judgment of the very experienced anthropologist, C. von Furer-Haimendorf, "thus arose a conflict between the traditional tribal ownership and the state's claim to the entire forest wealth."[7]

Nevertheless, as elsewhere, this was only the beginning of tribal disenfranchisement. The establishment of a Forest Department and reservation of large tracts of forest in Bastar were only part of the influx of new policies and new people. The "opening up and civilizing" of the kingdom drew a considerable contingent of opportunists—merchants, timber-traders, liquor-sellers, moneylenders, and land-hungry immigrants—who held in common a notion that the requirements of prosperity were not to be burdened with too great a load of absolute morality. Rather the opposite; what amounted to a very relativistic sense of morality encouraged the formation of a relationship between tribals and nontribals which was summed up by observers, including higher officials, in the dichotomy of the exploiter and the exploited. Over time this relationship developed a new set of vested interests which attenuated later attempts by the government to mitigate rapaciousness. As pointed out by von Furer-Haimendorf:

> Alienation of tribal lands cannot be prevented without depriving non-tribal landowners of the chance to enlarge their holdings, a curb on exploitation by money lenders interferes with the activities of local businessmen, and any attempt to eradicate corrupt practices of minor officials diminishes the income such persons are accustomed to derive from dealings with ignorant and illiterate tribals.[8]

Seen from this perspective, it is easily understood that the opposition generated by these vested interests to governmental ameliorative measures to rectify the exploiter-exploited relationship was generally great enough to render them mere palliatives. The feeble rhetoric of "uplift" prevailed. Extending the irony of the situation, some of the forest-protective measures introduced after Indian independence in 1948 even further expanded the opportunity for the exploitation of tribals.

From the late 1930s through the Bastar forestry project, officials have proposed experiments in which the Forest Department has assigned responsibility for trees or their products to tribal people. In the best of these experiments, tribal people have responded amid very fruitful signs that the government and tribals could cooperate in the forests. But concurrent processes have tended to undercut the potential of most of these experiments. The best account of the early cooperative forestry experiments in Bastar, written in 1974–1975 by Aurora and Reynolds, is based on and is in part a paraphrase of an unpublished 1952 report by R. Chakravarti:

> Co-operative forestry arrangements were instituted in Bastar in the late 1930s with remarkable success. Relatively heavy population densities around Jagdalpur town had in the late 1930s reduced much of the surrounding forest to scrubland by excessive cutting, unrestricted firing and excessive grazing. Faced with economic distress and physical destruction, the villagers and the administration came to a meeting of minds. They decided to introduce simple working schemes for the forest areas, the actual management of which was left in the hands of Panch Committees either elected or appointed by the villagers themselves. The results, according to the report, are "too good to be true."
>
> The tribals living around Jagdalpur town enjoyed certain rights to the protected forest area. They could take their bona fide requirements of firewood, bamboo, grass for grazing and minor forest projects. However, they were not conferred any proprietary or even user rights over these forests. Prima facie, the nistari forests were State property and the advantages to the villagers from these forests were in the nature of concessions which could at any time be modified, curtailed, or altogether withdrawn at the discretion of the administration. (More recently, the State has declared the nistari forests to be protected forests under Section 29 of the [1952] Indian Forest Act.)
>
> The Forest Department, in collaboration with the village leaders, devised two working schemes. The first, called the Ulnar Scheme, was designed for a block of about ten square miles of nistari forest situated ten miles east of Jagdalpur town. The forests under the scheme supplied the nistari demands

of 15 villages. The villages contained 1600 houses and more than 6,000 cattle. When the scheme was introduced in 1935 the forest was merely a scrub jungle with misshapen, unsound saplings and coppice shoots. Officials walked the whole area, examined the extent and condition of the forest, and ascertained the nistari and grazing requirements of the villages likely to benefit by the scheme. The forests were quickly demarcated, surveyed and mapped. A rough stock map was also prepared. It revealed that the area could easily be rehabilitated and a working scheme for 40 years was drawn up.

In essence the scheme was simple. The authorities realized that a complicated scheme may not be capable of being followed by the villagers. The forest was divided into eight felling series. Villages were allotted to each series in such a way that the villagers did not have to go far to obtain their requirement of forest produce. Each felling series was divided into 40 coupes of approximately equal area. One coupe was to be felled each year and the produce felled was to be divided among the villagers according to the nistari cess paid. After felling, the coupe was to be protected from fire and grazing for a period of five years. In the forty-first year, coupe number one, felled in the first year of working, would contain a forest mainly of coppice origin and would be ready for felling again. Trees yielding edible fruits or other minor forest produce of commercial importance such as harrar, mahua and imli were not to be felled. Trees held sacred by the villagers were similarly excluded from felling. Trees were to be felled flush with the ground so that good coppice shoots would be obtained. No fellings were to be carried out in areas outside the prescribed coupe for that year, except in a few special cases where the previous permission of the Panch had been obtained.

The actual working of the scheme was left in the hands of the villagers themselves. The Forest Department came into the picture ordinarily only once a year when the coupes were demarcated on the ground, and on occasions when other technical help was necessary or when there was a dispute over the working of the scheme. The management of the scheme was entrusted to a Panch of seven members elected by the villagers themselves. Members of the Panch in turn elected a chairman, the Sarpanch, to preside over the deliberations of the Panch. The Panch met once a week in the bazaar at Bajawand to discuss the working of the scheme and to transact other business as was entrusted to them. The protection of the forest against illicit felling and pilferage was in the hands of the Panch which appointed a rakhwar (guard) for each felling series. He was a whole-time servant of the scheme and it was his duty to patrol the forest regularly and to report cases of illicit fellings, illicit grazing, fire, etc., to the Panch. Where the offender was caught the rakhwar would produce him before the Panch. He also supervised the annual felling of the coupe and special fellings outside the coupe. For this service the rakhwar was paid roughly 80 lbs. of paddy per month. He was also supplied with a uniform and an axe.

The scheme was financed by each village in relation to its land revenue assessment. The village Ulnar, which paid a land revenue of Rs. 1,192, contributed 1,192 pailies of paddy to the scheme. [1 pailie = 4 lbs. of paddy/rice.] From the paddy so collected the Panch paid the rakhwar. The surplus paddy was sold and the proceeds were used to purchase uniforms and other incidental expenses connected with the working of the scheme.

The Panch was invested with certain powers. It tried offenders in cases of illicit fellings, theft, etc., and could impose fines to the extent of Rs. 25 in each case. It appointed and dismissed the rakhwars. The Panch in effect was the supreme authority insofar as the working of the scheme was concerned. No appeal against the decision of the Panch could be made except in a few cases where the administration could interfere if it believed that the decision of the Panch had been perverse or not fair and just. The fines collected from forest offence cases were credited by the Panch to the general fund of the schemes and were utilized for the furtherance of the scheme.

Eight villages participated in the Ulnar scheme. The acreage involved per village varied from 500 to 1200 acres.

At the time of the preparation of the Ulnar scheme village rights to forest land were governed by a complicated relationship to ceremonial worship. Nonetheless, the Forest Department was able to demarcate forest land in relation to the village without any problem. Today the traditional ceremonial system, called Saridodi, may not hold or may have altered in form. Whatever, there is no reason to assume that it would prove an obstacle.

The Ulnar scheme had been in operation for 16 years at the time of the report. The results achieved were described as "too good to be true" and the report claimed that full justice could not be done by setting them down on paper. The report claimed, "the coupes have regenerated very well and contain fine young stands of Sal. The coupes still to be felled have escaped the wanton use of the axe for 16 years and responded wonderfully to protection. The villagers now have a piece of forest which will meet their nistari requirements in perpetuity on the principle of sustained yield. The Panch has been fully alive to its responsibilities and has run the scheme smoothly and successfully all these years. There have been no serious cases of dispute and the administration has practically never been called upon to interfere. A 'people's forest has been created, worked by the people and for the people.' "

Later, in 1941, the Madhota scheme was drawn up for 7,500 acres to meet the nistari demands of 21 villages, again near Jagdalpur. The scheme was similar in all general principles to the Ulnar scheme. The main difference was that the area contained two types of forest: one Sal and one predominantly miscellaneous species. The two types of forest were worked separately within one plan. Thus the Madhota scheme provided not only for fruit trees to be preserved against felling but also allowed for the development of valuable timber.[9]

These two schemes continued successfully until their "demise" about 1952 when, following Indian independence, a new Forest Act was instituted which spurred renewal of Forest Department interest in revenue performance. A second and very significant reason for the demise of cooperative forestry in Bastar has to do with its tradition of leadership—the monarchy—and how its replacement was mishandled by the Government of India in a series of events to be described in chapter seven. Suffice it to say here that the imposition of "official" village leaders, replacing those whose allegiance was to the Maharaja of Bastar, led to the severe neglect of cooperative forestry. These new leaders lacked a stake in cooperative forestry and may be presumed to have represented, at the village level, the demand for increased revenue embodied in 1952 forest policy. Such a demand on forests was not new: just ten years earlier, during the war, the first commercial teak plantations had been established in Bastar on 19,500 hectares (although not in one location). In total area, however, this teak plantation was almost as large as the Caribbean pine plantation would have been.

The national forest policy, the present Forest Act of 1952, exemplified the paradoxical nature of growing government intervention. The impetus for the new policy came from and reflected the vigorous nationalism occasioned by the achievement of independence. The princely states were completely assimilated into the Indian Union and the feudal orders, which had been only partially subservient to British paramount authority, were abolished. New forest policies had to be devised to articulate the changeover to nationalistic priorities. These are clearly set out in the following official Indian government statement:

Village Communities in the neighbourhood of a forest will naturally make greater use of its products for the satisfaction of their domestic and agricultural needs. Such use, however, should in no event be permitted at the cost of national interests. *The accident of a village being situated close to a forest does not prejudice the right of the country as a whole to receive benefits of a national asset.* The scientific conservation of a forest inevitably involves the regulation of rights and the restriction of the privilege of users depending upon the value and importance of the forest, however irksome such restraint may be to the neighbouring areas. . . . While, therefore, the needs of the local population must be met to a reasonable extent, national interests should not be sacrificed because they are not directly discernible, nor should the rights and interests of future generations be subordinated to the improvidence of the present generation [emphasis added].[10]

Thus it became firmly established that "tribal villages were no longer an essential part of the forests but were there merely on sufferance. The traditional rights of the tribals were no longer recognized as rights. In 1894 they became 'rights and privileges' and in 1952 they became 'rights and concessions'. Now (1963) they are regarded as concessions."[11] Nonetheless, the British protectionist attitudes toward the tribals—as a result of realizing the ill effects of "civilization"—were to some degree retained.

As part of the 1952 policy changes implemented in the newly created district of Bastar, the tribals were allotted small areas of forest (village forests) over which they were formally assigned ownership. Unfortunately, the concept of private ownership was more or less a novelty in the barely monetized economy of tribal people; the advantageous implications of this were readily grasped by immigrant timber contractors. Contractors' activities between the early 1950s and the mid-1970s gave rise to the *malik makbooja* system, a colloquial term signifying the sale and purchase by private contractors of trees owned by individual tribals. In 1957 it became legal for tribals to convert rights to land, but not to timber standing on it (*bhumadari* rights) into rights to both the land and its timber (*bhumaswami* rights) upon payment of a sum equal to three times the annual land revenue. A large amount of land acquired by tribals this way was subsequently alienated from them. The abuses of this system produced enormous profits for the contractors. Unfortunately the "Protection of Tribal Interest in Trees Act of 1959," promulgated to ensure administrative supervision and regulation of sales, had little corrective effect. The lower echelons of the local bureaucracy were merely further drawn by this legislation into corrupt manipulations. The profits from reselling trees for Rs 200 to 300 (around $40 U.S.) which had been bought for as little as Rs 5 (about 60 cents U.S.) per tree stimulated a host of ingenuities designed to circumvent the rigorous enforcement of forest law.[12] The complete reorganization of the Forest Department in 1976, designed to eliminate all of this, simply changed its pattern.

Events such as these evince the ironic and contradictory historical progression of the mismanagement of tribal/nontribal relations. In Bastar, initially, the overzealous application of arbitrary authority in regard to tribal forests produced a reaction strong enough to be called a rebellion. Later ameliorative modifications to that authority were so little enforced as to allow massive exploitation of tribal rights. As Jones points out in respect to the tribal situation in general:

> Perhaps the most crucial prerequisite for tribal development is to curb severely the power of the non-tribal money lenders, landlords and traders that control the tribal economy. However, since the political organisers for the centre and centre-right parties that are likely to control any government under the present political system come from this class it is highly unlikely that this basic change will ever be made. The laws exist, but no government that wants to remain in power can afford to implement them.[13]

With equal cogency this applies to the forest situation in Bastar. It is hardly surprising that the forest officials and tribal people in Bastar find themselves in an antagonistic atmosphere of suspicion and mistrust.[14] From the tribal perspective, the latter attitudes are extended to virtually all outsiders.

The various forest acts and codes constitute a kind of fault line in government-tribal relations. Tribal violations and the consequent penalties are an index of the tension along this fault line. Standard fines and penalties can be levied, or not, at the discretion of the officers of the Forest Department. In 1978, for example, forestry plantation and protection officers explained that they had received letters right down at the operative level from the highest officials of the Forest Department instructing them to produce more revenue. The same pressure has been repeatedly conveyed in the monthly meetings of range officers, always in the same form: "Range X has contributed (a stated amount of revenue) and Range Y is not contributing enough." Before an election, according to these plantation and protection officers, it is common for a Minister to order that the forests be opened for nistari for both tribals and nontribals without penalty. But after the election, the same Minister is likely to demand more revenue from the same forest. Part of the revenue can be generated through fines, such as for illegal cutting or hunting. At the same time, the same officers can earn unrecorded private income when they agree to lower a fine at their own discretion, or "not file a POR (preliminary offence report) this time." As unrecorded income can also be produced through "harassment"—a term used in all official reports on tribal relations with the government— there is considerable scope for private income among government staff, from forest guards right up to the highest officers who regulate the private forestry contractors.

But even where the squeeze for unreported income is not the main issue, the curtailment of customary tribal expectations by the Forest Department leads to annoyance and humiliation. *Parhat* (ritual hunting) is a useful example. In January 1978 a *patel* (village headman) near Geedam was, with other men of his village, conducting parhat on the most auspicious day of the year. The group was caught with two chital deer and fined Rs 500, although the maximum allowable fine was Rs 2,000 in this case. The confiscated deer were then auctioned back to the hunting group. Because it was their kill, because they had to produce the deer at home for ritual reasons, and because the meat was still fresh, they paid for the auctioned deer. But they did not pay the fine. In a letter to the district commissioner, in English, the patel himself took responsibility for the group's violation of the law. He then said: "We do not mind the fine so much as we mind the contempt of the government for our tradition [of parhat]. We are responsible to the government as citizens, but the government is also responsible to us." Two months after the incident, the fine had not been paid. The range officers of the Forest Department explained that after about ten days they would take the patel to court, where he has ultimately paid other such fines in the past. "We could easily send him to jail," they said, "but we just don't do that."

This example illustrates one source of tribal mistrust of government undertakings. Individuals are apprehended for carrying out their cultural duties. The sacred and illegal deer are bought back, for a recorded and unrecorded sum, and the festival continues. They petition the highest government officer (equivalent in rank to the king) regarding the indignity of this incident, and though the fine may be further commuted, they will have to pay something, to someone, in addition to having experienced prolonged annoyance and inconvenience.

In 1978 Robert Anderson was given the following list of forest income sources for tribals:

1. Sale of mahua flowers or seeds for liquor preparation. Excise department restricts the amount in possession.

2. Sale of mahua seed kernels for oil.

3. Sale of tendu patta (leaves for bidi cigarettes) at rates fixed by the Forest Department.

4. Sale of sal seed and resin; under permission of Forest Department, which sells in turn at auction to highest bidder.

5. Sale of gum; harrar (*myrobolams* for extracting tannin used in ink, medicine, leather tanning).

6. Sale of silk cocoons.

7. Sale of honey and beeswax.

8. Sale of tamarind seed.

9. Sale of firewood and grass.

10. Wages for timber-felling—on day-rate or piece-rate basis.

11. Wages for bamboo-cutting.

12. Sale of bamboo products made from by-products of bamboo-cutting activities (sale of these products unofficial, but conducted within the sight of officials).

At the same time the Forest Department obtained official revenue from the forests on the basis of four main sources:

1. Sale proceeds of all products (now nationalized).

2. Compensation for leasing out land under its control (e.g., the Bailadila iron ore mine, or the forestry development corporation plantation land).

3. Fines arising from violation of the Forest Act (e.g., hunting animals or illegal cutting).

4. Charges for removal of forest products allowed by nistari rights, such as dead fuel (Rs 1 per cartload official rate; unofficial rates about Rs 6).

In current practice, three other government departments obtain indirect revenue from the forests: the revenue, excise, and sales tax departments. This extraction does not include the unofficial and unreported incomes of contractors and officials in a number of departments.

Compared with the Forest Department, tribal involvement is pervasive to a profound degree. The mahua tree will serve as an example. In addition to collecting flowers and seeds for sale at the weekly market, or for exchange for salt or cloth, tribals use the wood to support the canopy at wedding celebrations, the dried flower to add bulk to their food or to feed their animals, the seeds and the flowers for preparing liquor and for religious ceremonies. Finally, not only in life but also in death the tribals are integrated with the forests. Those who have cremations do so in the forest, using many forest products in the ritual. Those who have burials locate their cemeteries deep in the forest. In both instances, big wooden posts are erected as memorials. Like all others, Bastar tribals have been particularly sensitive about desecration of their sacred grounds. The forests do not appear to them merely in terms of economic usefulness.

This pattern is extended to every minor forest product, to every extra load of bamboo, because the forest codes and regulations specify every concession to the tribals and limit each one. The authority of the Forest Department, and its ultimate coercive power, is thus manifest almost everywhere to the tribals. To the tribals, an industrial forestry project that undermines the habitat of wildlife, eliminates some desirable species of trees, and pushes minor forest products farther and farther from their villages becomes immediately suspect. The probability of violations of the regulations, in such circumstances, might well increase. The tension along this fault line might certainly give way to violence, as it did in 1982, with reports of confrontations between tribals and the government. The Forest Department is, after all, a paramilitary operation in these matters: it has policing powers and frequently finds it must use them. The occasional murder of a forest guard during the World Bank's project—and its contribution to this tension—did not go unnoticed. Tribal involvement in crime was on the increase in Dantewada tehsil at the time of the Bailadila massacre in 1978, as we shall see. It is reasonable to expect repetition of this trend in the context of an industrial forestry project, where interference in the status quo is not limited to a hole in the ground, but is to be found in every glade of the forest.[15]

From the perspective of forest officials, the tribal is seen as an incorrigible destroyer of forest wealth, an irremediable "primitive" whose innate weaknesses can only be expected to be exploited. In the opinion of one Bastar divisional forest officer, "It is the human tendency that, if unchecked, strong tries to exploit the week [sic]."[16] Another report states that it is necessary to "enforce benevolent compulsion on the people to curb their instinctive urge to destroy forests."[17] The controversy over the tribal destruction of forests is an old and unresolved one. Many foresters in India, and elsewhere, consider all swidden cultivation negatively. It is clear, though, that within certain population densities and rotation cycles, swidden practices are not ecologically destructive. It is also a fact, in Bastar, that higher population densities correlate with a greater emphasis on permanent plough cultivation. And then there are the reactions of tribal people themselves, who counter "by asking how they *could* destroy the forest." As they pointed out:

> They owned no trucks; they hardly had even a bullock-cart; the utmost that they could carry away was a headload of produce for sale to maintain their families and that too against a licence. The utmost that they wanted was wood to keep them warm in the winter months, to reconstruct or repair their huts and carry on their little cottage industries. Their fuel-needs for cooking, they said, were not much, because they had not much to cook. Having explained their own position they invariably turned to the amount the ex-zamindars (feudal lease-holders), in violation of their agreements and the forest rules and laws, devastated vast areas of forest land right in front of officials. . . . There is a feeling amongst the tribals that all the arguments in support of preservation and development of forest are intended to refuse them their demands. They argue that when it is a question of industry, township, development work or projects of rehabilitation, all these plausible arguments are forgotten and vast tracts are placed at the disposal of outsiders who mercilessly destroy the forest wealth with or without necessity.[18]

Perhaps it is needless to say that these arguments and those of the forest officials are extreme characterizations. They do, nevertheless, mark the polemical boundaries of tribal-Forest Department relations.[19] They also indicate the mutually opposed definitions held by the two groups. It is remarkable that the situation in essence is still as it was in 1853: one of "civilization" versus "savagery." With these definitions of the situation, the planning of the Bastar forestry project began in the early 1970s.

Muria headman shaping a hiking staff for one of the authors. This village is many miles from the nearest road. The wood was taken from a tribally owned and managed forest in the Abujhmar. Muria values have produced a strategy which gives them continuous and balanced access to forest resources. (W. Huber photo)

Two diffident Hill Maria men attending a major market at Narayanpur. As a result of long-standing, protectionist, local administrative policy (recently dropped), the Hill Maria are the only group whose economy remains firmly based on swidden cultivation. Their habitat, the Abujhmar, has been described by biologists as the last truly wild biosphere in peninsular India. For various reasons, including a number of large dam projects, its future as such is now coming under serious doubt. This has already attracted the attention of an incipient environmental movement in India. (W. Huber photo)

Best known for their co-ed youth dormitories, these Muria sell their few vegetables at the weekly market, an integrative institution at the economic interface of Gond and Hindu societies in Bastar. For most tribal participants, however, the weekly market encompasses more social and cultural than economic activity. Nevertheless, these markets form the primary outlets for the sale of gathered "minor forest products," which are resold by nontribal middlemen and contractors for up to ten times the purchase price. The nationalization of "MFPs" has altered these transactions only in the somewhat reduced degree of mark-up. (W. Huber photo)

The Madhya Pradesh Forestry Technical Assistance Project reception and the guest house at Kurundi, about 7 kms. east of Jagdalpur. The pine project facilities, such as this one and the newly constructed offices and residences in Jagdalpur itself, now stand abandoned. The original offices, on the other hand, have been taken over by the Mining Corporation of India as part of a dolomite extraction project in the selfsame Kurundi area. In the summer of 1985 tribal protest, again founded on loss of forest use, was threatening this project as well. (W. Huber photo)

Pinus caribaea at the defunct Kurundi nursery. The first *P. caribaea* were planted in Bastar in 1968. Planting was stopped suddenly in 1974, but revived in 1976 with the World Bank loan. By 1980 survival rates were reported to be very uneven, and significantly lower than 76 percent — in some areas the new trees experienced 50 percent mortality, and many other trees showed immature growth. (W. Huber photo)

Scaling logs on top of a truck in Jagdalpur. Under a reorganization of the Forestry Department in Bastar, a production forestry unit has been added to the department's conservation staff. This has resulted in an unprecedented amount of commercial logging in the district. According to a recent report Bastar has the biggest timber depot in Asia with an average auction value of over US$8 million. (W. Huber photo)

Interior forest access road during monsoon, a period of impassability lasting nearly six months in the more remote parts of Bastar. In 1984 the chairman of the Bastar Tribal Development Authority stated that the top planning priority needed to be given to communications, especially road building, since this deficiency was "the main reason for exploitation of tribal people." It is interesting to note that traditional tribal settlement patterns reveal a tendency to locate away from main roads, indicating quite the reverse perception. (W. Huber photo)

Tribal village in north-central Bastar. The trees in the background and much of the forests between villages in this area are tribally owned. A partial list of forest products used in, or gathered by the inhabitants of, such villages would include house timbers, roof thatching, fence posts, shaped lumber for agricultural (plows) and kitchen use (rice pounders), fuelwood; edible produce such as tamarinds, bamboo shoots, wild mangos and figs, mahua flowers (for liquor distillation), mahua and sal *(Shorea robusta)* seeds for cooking oil, wild honey, and a number of other wild-growing roots and tubers; commercial products such as *tassar* silk cocoons, lac, *harrar* (myrobalams for extracting tannin used in ink, medicine, and leather tanning), beeswax, and *tendu patta*, the leaves of the ebony tree used in the manufacture of bidis, the "poor man's" cigarette of India. (W. Huber photo)

Muria men enjoying "sulphi" wine (similar to palm wine) on the way home from the weekly market. Conversations are rich and poetic. News about the pine plantations was typically communicated among tribal people on market day. (W. Huber photo)

Billboard in the town of Jagdalpur, this one reading "Protect the Forest from Fire," and showing a tribal man setting fire to a forest in "this birth" and being roasted over a fire in "hell." From the perspective of forest officials, the tribal is seen as an incorrigible destroyer of forest wealth, an irremediable "primitive" whose destructive instincts can be curbed only by the harshest coercion. (W. Huber photo)

Offices of the Conservator of Forests in Jagdalpur. In 1982, an environmental study group from Bhopal visited the office to find out what forces were responsible for the large-scale felling of forests in the district. Reported Anil Sadgopal: "Of course, the Chief Conservator said the tribals . . . were burning fuelwood, building houses with the wood, stealing bamboo, and taking more than the allowed headload of timber. And we found, to our surprise, that a Hyderabad-based company was making a certain kind of steel for which it needed coal. To make the coal it had undertaken a large-scale contract, using wood from the forests of Bastar. We found that the amount of wood this company was using for making steel was more than the total amount of fuelwood used by the Adivasis in that district; yet this fact will never be revealed to you by the forest authorities." The men in the foreground are collecting water from a public tap. (W. Huber photo)

Pravir Chandra Bhanj Deo (1929–1966), Maharajah of Bastar, photographed circa 1958. His family was not originally from Bastar, but was adopted by tribal people as their rulers. With the progressive dissolution of these monarchies after 1947, Pravir tried to maintain some independence from Delhi (where he was thought to be an eccentric nuisance). He was killed in 1966 by police during a public confrontation.

The Remawand (Muria) gotul putting on a dance for visitors. Note the large stack of firewood at left: it is obligatory for gotul residents to add to it daily. Wood and products from different trees have dozens of practical and ceremonial uses in daily life. A pine monoculture would have changed all that. (W. Huber photo)

A rare photograph of Baba Bihari Dass, the holy man who became a leader of Bastar tribal people after the shooting of the Maharajah in 1966 by skillfully using his perceived links to the dead ruler. He is shown (in 1978) seated among his followers beside the water tank at his headquarters at Chapka, shortly after his release from prison. His critique of the pine project was communicated throughout Bastar and may have influenced even those who were not his loyal followers.

Woman watering Caribbean pine seedlings in the Madhya Pradesh Forestry Development Corporation nursery. This was designated by tribal people as work suitable for women—men were felling the existing forest to make space for the plantations. Other cash employment was on irrigation, road work, and iron ore mining. Continued work in pine plantations was not rated highly by tribal people during a 1980 government study.

Rice field in valley with watch tower—a typical landscape with forest-covered hills and valley-bottom rice cultivation in central Bastar. The tower allows farmers to sleep near the field at harvest time safe from predatory animals. Forest products are close at hand. (W. Huber photo)

CHAPTER 4

Plans for Industrial Forestry

Different segments of the tribal population of Bastar today are at different stages of assimilation with the more advanced mainstream of Indian culture. The complexity of the social situation in Bastar would call, therefore, for a fairly sophisticated social engineering. —Ford Foundation study, 1976

GIVEN the complex matrix of state, private, and tribal interests in the forests—including competing definitions of the trees and the rights of access to them—an extremely tough test of the relation between ideas for development and institutional practices occurred from 1976 through 1981. These were the years in which industrial development was planned for Bastar forests.

The plans made were intended ultimately to transform the biological environment by reducing the genetic diversity, the sociological environment by changing the demographic balance away from the tribals, and the administrative environment by modifying the state supervision of forestry operations. Given these planned changes, could significant communication be created between the state, private sector, and tribals about their competing definitions and expectations? Could scientific expertise be applied successfully to this question? Would the international agencies that guide and underwrite part of the cost of India's development play a leading role in creating significant communication about the forests?

When the International Development Association (IDA) loan was made to India in 1975 for a Technical Assistance Project (TAP) to determine the feasibility of a commercial pulp and paper mill in Bastar, the World Bank was acting on advice accumulated during the previous one hundred years. Since the first appearance of reports and books by officials about forestry or Bastar, the potential for commercial forestry had been proclaimed over and over again. The railways and highways into and through Bastar, linking it to the coast and to the rest of the state

51

MAHARASHTRA

BASTAR DISTRICT

MADHYA
PRADESH

UNMANAGED
TRIBAL
FOREST

NARAYANPUR

KONDAGAON

JAGDALPUR
CATCHMENT

ORISSA

BARSUR
CATCHMENT

Indravati

River

BARSUR

GEEDAM

JAGDALPUR

KURUNDI
PILOT PINE
PLANTATION
AREA

W. BASTAR

BIJAPUR

DANTEWARA

BAILADILA

KIRANDUL

CATCHMENT

STEEP FOREST
AREA

Godavari

Sabari

River

N

ANDHRA   PRADESH

River

0   20   40 km

INDIA

BASTAR
DISTRICT

Arabian
Sea

Bay of Bengal

0   400 km

**INDUSTRIAL FORESTRY MAP FOR
BASTAR TECHNICAL ASSISTANCE PROJECT**

Bay of
Bengal

After IBRD 11730, 1975

Of Bastar's total area of 39,060 km², 21,700 km² were under control of the state Forest Department during the pine project. Nearly all of the districts's tropical, moist deciduous forests, composed of over 100 species, mainly teak, sal *(Shorea robusta)* and laurel, were thus subject to departmental control and classification. The Forestry Development Corporation planned pine plantations in the Barsur and West Bastar catchment areas. The Kurundi area near Jagdalpur was the original site for *Pinus caribaea* trials begun in 1968.

of Madhya Pradesh, were specifically intended for the extraction of timber and consequent increased revenue. Extraction and revenue have been the responsibility of one of the largest and most powerful government departments, the Forest Department of Madhya Pradesh. Sometimes the responsibility has been indirect, shared with contractors and other government departments. But before the Bastar project began, the responsibility had become direct, and government officials experienced tension and confusion in the new situation.

A kind of self-evaluation of the recent history and objectives of the Forest Department can be found in the 1976 *Souvenir*, written by the senior officials of the department (chief conservators, deputy conservators, conservator-in-chief, special secretary of the finance department, secretary to the environment group of departments, director of the state forest research institute, project manager of the Bastar TAP, managing director of the state forestry development corporation, et al.).[1] Most important, the department experienced two profound changes shortly before the Bastar project began—the complete nationalization of all forest products, and the complete reorganization of the bureaucratic setup. Prior to these changes, officials wrote, foresters had first been "devoted conservationists" concerned with regulatory control, not exploitation of the forests. This began to change as the demand for more revenue penetrated the working ethos: foresters were described as more like "careerists" whose work tended to dilute their commitment to conservation. These two tendencies produced "a kind of schizophrenia" in foresters, said the *Souvenir*. Some foresters were less committed to conservation than others. Revenue demands culminated in nationalization and total control: in 1965 the lucrative tendu patta business (leaves for bidi cigarettes) was nationalized; timber was brought under control in 1972, bamboo, in 1973. The objective, officials wrote, was to "eliminate pilferage and theft" and to secure maximum government revenues.

The consequences of nationalization were to bring about a 200 percent increase in forest revenue between 1965 and 1975. Middlemen and contractors, the scourge of both the Forest Department and tribal people, were eliminated. Some of the forest products with low costs of maintenance and harvesting (such as bamboo) became "highly profitable," said the *Souvenir.* The department bought some forest products cheaply and sold them dearly, as the middlemen had always done. Yet the fact remained that field staff were "torn between proper management and maximizing revenue." Indeed, noticed some, increased revenue derived not from an increase in yield per hectare, but simply from a "change in the system of exploitation." Clearly something different was required. Reorganization began in 1976, along with the start of the World Bank project.

The state was divided into an east and west sector, each with three new divisions—for "protection", "exploitation," and "marketing." Each division would be evaluated by separate criteria, and all would report to the same departmental headquarters in Bhopal. The political leaders, including the Chief Minister, and Minister of Forests, were reportedly enthusiastic about the new setup. The objective, officials wrote just after the reorganization, was again "the complete elimination of illicit felling and theft." Also supposed to disappear, through the separation of the protection and exploitation functions, was the schizophrenia noted earlier. Nevertheless, "a certain amount of friction" was expected between the new divisions, so the conservator-in-chief would have to balance the reliance upon their separate operating criteria.

In spite of the dramatic increase in forest revenue, officials wrote that the department deserved "better treatment": although contributing between 14 and 18 percent of the state's gross revenue, it was allocated only 1 percent of the state's budget in 1976. (Inconsistencies between accounts of revenue offered by government officials in the *Souvenir* thwart the attempt to assess the revenue picture in 1975–1976. In that year the Forest Department contributed between 14 and 18 percent of the revenue of Madhya Pradesh. This contribution had been roughly constant for the preceding six years. In 1975–1976 forestry contributed 55 percent of Madhya Pradesh's nontax revenue, according to the Forest Department.) Quadrupling revenue in the previous ten years had aggravated the situation within the department: it is hard to see how the schizophrenia would really diminish. Foresters were bitter that although their work was valuable, they were largely disregarded at budget allocation time. The key to better treatment—"the silver lining" one called it—was held by the new forestry development corporation, empowered by a new state Act to capture more of the revenue generated in the forests and reinvest it. But the corporation was totally committed to exploitation. Said its two most senior officers, "We cannot lock up our resources for long ventures and forest resources have to be mobilized more rapidly." Others in the department, saying that policy makers "exaggerate the importance of short-term resources," stressed the need for research and careful evaluation of alternate schemes, including quick rotation plantations. These doubts, expressed in the *Souvenir*, continued throughout the period of the Bastar project, probably contributing to its termination in 1981. The debate among foresters all over the world can be read in the *Commonwealth Forestry Review* or the *FAO News* for Asia and the Pacific: it should not be presumed that they spoke with one voice.

The Bastar project was based on a lengthy history of studies and reports, beginning with the preinvestment survey of forest resources during the Third Five-Year Plan from 1961 to 1966 to determine industrial catchment areas. Conditions were so favorable that the World Bank sent an appraisal mission in 1964, which recommended a 100,000 ton per annum pulp mill for Bastar. Between 1964 and 1968 a number of studies were done under a joint United Nations and Government of India project: these included the Nagaraj Committee report, the Le Cacheux report, and studies by international consulting firms. Proposals were made for a smaller 50,000–100,000 ton mill. The United Nations Development Program carried out the first complete photographic survey of Bastar forests in 1966, the first of many before the advent of LANDSAT satellite imagery, which was used in Bastar in the late 1970s.[2] In 1968 Caribbean pines were first grown in Bastar. The Commonwealth Scientific and Industrial Research Organization (CSIRO) of Australia and a Canadian dissolving-pulp specialist studied the district's potential, and from then on greater commitment was made and more detailed planning was done.

A major step occurred in 1970 when the Marketing and Research Corporation of India studied the whole Indian potential for wood and wood products. This study identified Bastar as a prime source of exports within a decade. The study concluded that there would not likely be any decline in world paper prices, and that, indeed, a price rise beyond 1975 seemed certain. Moreover, major manufacturing countries could not compete favorably against India if export strategies were "pursued promptly and with a single mind."[3] But the problem lay in supply of wood. Between 1970 and 1980 there would be a shortage of bamboo, and present cutting of coniferous species could not meet the need for long-fibered pulp to improve paper quality. Eucalyptus would

TABLE 3
Comparison of Cost (rupees per cubic foot) of
Delivered Pulpwood, Including Royalties (ranked), 1970

Florida (hardwood)	1.50
Bastar (bamboo)	1.80
Quebec (hardwood)	1.80
South Carolina (pine)	1.89
Bastar (hardwood)	1.95
Florida (pine)	2.10
Eastern Canada (softwood)	2.70–3.00

Source: Marketing and Research Corporation of India, 1970. (These prices were one basis for the decision to plan the Bastar pine plantation project.)

come onstream only in the 1980s. Bagasse was available, but was largely unproven as a source of paper. Fortunately, said the study, "no shortage of tropical hardwoods will hinder production programs for pulp and paper during the next decade."[4] But following 1980, tropical pines could be substituted if a yield of 15 cubic meters per hectare in a thirty-year cutting cycle could be maintained: "This provides the major long-run solution to India's serious shortage," said the study, but not for at least ten years.[5] The study then compared the projected cost of Bastar pulp wood with other significant current markets (see table 3) and decided it could compete well if delivered in Hong Kong and the Middle East.

Social Assumptions of Preliminary Studies

Eleven studies were done in Bastar forests between 1964 and 1974, but two industrial plans—by Tewari and Susaeta in 1973 and by Tewari in 1974—were largely the basis of the World Bank's loan: the assumptions of these two studies, therefore, are very important to assess with respect to the social impact of the industrial forestry project.

Eladio Susaeta, attached to the Ford Foundation and the Planning Commission of India, and D. N. Tewari, with the Madhya Pradesh

Forest Department, concluded in 1973 that although "a large majority of the cultivators need to supplement their meagre agricultural income through alternative employment," there would still be a need for migratory forest workers.[6] They described the district's labor force in the following terms: in 1971 there were estimated to be 511,000 workers (77 percent male and 23 percent female), of whom 317,000 were owner-cultivators of land; 128,000 were agricultural and forestry workers; and 66,000 were industrial, mining, and domestic workers. Without knowing how big the forestry development would be, they concluded that "today's local labour force will not suffice to man the project."[7] Acknowledging that tribals made up a part of this work force, they opined that "impoverished tribals will get concrete possibilities of improving their lot *without abandoning their traditional physical environment*. This will alleviate the social problems hitherto experienced with the Bailadila area of this project" (emphasis in original).[8]

The serious social effects of the first big Bastar industrial project—the Bailadila mine, which had contracted to ship iron ore to Japan—were already known in 1973. Tribal men were not included in the mine's employment force, except as casual laborers, and tribal women worked in the area only as domestic servants and, in some cases, as prostitutes. These facts formed part of the oral history of the industrial forest project. How the tribals would actually be included in the forest project was not addressed by Tewari and Susaeta; they simply offered the hope that, because the project would be in the forests, tribals would be employed.

In his 1974 report, Tewari, then the deputy conservator of forests in Madhya Pradesh, spelled out his department's view of the history of the tribals' use of the forests and the potential relation of their lives to industrial forestry. In an admixture of description and prescription, Tewari explained that "the poor infrastructure facilities, the preponderance of tribal population, lack of any purposive, positive and effective policy aimed at bringing about all-round development of this region till recently all have contributed to the present backwardness of the district."[9] "Forestry operations are mainly performed by tribals."[10] Before the government had begun to manage the forests, he wrote erroneously, "the people were free to settle anywhere they liked and could fell any forest for any purpose."[11] This had been stopped, fortunately, and now the problem was that "tribals are mainly poor, primitive and illiterate. The self-contained socio-economic system of these people today faces the prospect of merging itself into the forward-looking competitive fast-moving egalitarian way of life. . . . Under these circumstances the fate of tribals and that of forest development is inextricably linked."[12]

And of what advantage would industrial forestry be to Bastar? Employment, said Tewari. Although the supply of laborers in the off-season (from November to May) was adequate, for the rest of the year Bastar had to draw upon the neighboring districts of Madhya Pradesh, Orissa, and Andhra Pradesh, where there were "generous" labor surpluses.

> Migratory labourers are gaining popularity all over the country. Labour management is slowly entering all the departments and the forest department cannot be an exception to this change. Besides arranging labour gangs it shall be worthwhile to make provision for camping facilities, payment of advances, jobs for longer periods at one place, and allotment of work according to working ability and aptitude.[13]

The aptitude question arose for migrant laborers because of the unskilled nature of the tribals: Tewari explained that one of the advantages of the project was that "the implementation of a scheme such as this will provide *concrete economic support in their traditional environment*" (emphasis in original).[14] In the unwritten history of the project, tribals were expected by various officials to do unskilled work in the bush or in the loading yards—all low-paid and low-status roles. Beyond this kind of employment, Tewari predicted that the improved infrastructure of paved roads "shall result in the socio-economic development of the tribals." Further, their home fuel costs would decrease: "Delivery of increased quantity of lower dimension wood at lower cost would reduce the sale prices in local markets, which shall be a great relief to the tribals, the weakest link in our society."[15] But although tribals sold to local firewood markets, they did not buy from them. State control of these markets, and supposed lower prices, would probably work to their economic disadvantage. (See table 1, p. 8.)

Key Provisions of the World Bank Loan

The 1975 project document notes that although 23 percent of the total land surface of India is designated forest, in the early 1970s forestry and logging provided employment for only 0.2 percent of the labor force and contributed only 1.3 percent of the GNP of India as compared with agriculture, which contributed 45 percent. This may be misleading, however, if one concludes that the forests were economically unimportant: the statistics are perhaps unrealistic. For example, 371,000 are recorded employed as "forest product workers" in 1978, but millions depended on the forests. In any case, the World Bank believed this situation should be improved. India's need for foreign exchange, as well as for increased employment, had also led to the Bastar project. The Bank documents explained that India needed foreign exchange to service its massive external public debt—$12.4 billion—almost half of it borrowed from the World Bank and the International Monetary Fund (IMF). In addition, due to oil price increases, the Bank predicted a balance of payments deficit of $2.4 or $2.5 billion for India in 1975–1976. With these facts in mind, Bank forestry missions visited Bastar in 1974 and 1975 to assess the conditions described by Tewari and Susaeta. These missions concluded that "the present growth rate using natural regeneration of the vast Bastar forests is only two to three thousand hectares per year and included a wide range of species, some of which are of marginal value. With reforestation using fast-growing industrial species, the same forest areas would yield 10 to 15 thousand hectares per year of wholly usable wood": regrowth would thus jump up to five times the present rates.[16]

As a result of these missions, the World Bank and the Government of India agreed to a five-year project, which, if successful, would ultimately transform the biological, sociological, and legal-administrative environments in Bastar. First of all, large areas of Bastar were to be clear-cut and pilot plantation experiments carried out on pines (mainly *Pinus caribaea*), eucalyptus, and gmelina. A later FAO mission to Bastar described the problem of "a wide diversity of presently unmarketable species." By the end of the five-year project (1976–1980), 3,100 hectares were supposed to be under pilot plantations. If these were successful, the complexity of the forest could be reduced to fewer than three long-fibered industrial species suitable for pulp and paper production. The effect on coexistent flora and fauna would be profound. The Bank document called it "monoculture"; in effect, the presently intact forests would become gigantic plantations.[17]

Along with the biological transformation would come a remarkable change in society. Because the rate of regeneration would increase, so would the rate of extraction. In fact, the rate of extraction of the existing forest would have to increase dramatically above present cutting rates simply to allow for expansion of the plantation system. Enormous employment possibilities were anticipated. The proper management of the enlarged labor force was to be studied, including the participation of the tribals. Not only would there be a larger nontribal population in Bastar, but it would also live more deeply than ever before in exclusively tribal areas. The spatial order would be changed. Therefore, a major "study of tribals" was announced as part of the agreement, to devise complementary schemes to create employment opportunities for tribals, and to bring the nistari forests (in which tribals have concessions) under "controlled management" thereby "preserving the reserved forests for commercial timber production."[18] All of this would be done to "strike a balance between the claims for industrial wood production and the customary rights of local users."

Finally, a complex legal and administrative change was planned in the Bank's document. Both reserved and protected forests would be made inaccessible except for commercial harvest of the desired species. To make this simplification possible, the existing hardwood forest was to be cut and sold. But how could the proceeds of this sale be captured for reinvestment? The Bank and the Government of India agreed to create the Madhya Pradesh Forestry Development Corporation (MPFDC), which would in turn enjoy special amendments to the tax regulations, allowing it to offset against revenue the establishment costs of reforestation and to amortize certain costs (e.g., road construction). Since the revenue from sale of timber stock would determine cash flow, said the document, the tax regulations had to be favorably amended—and they were.[19] Revenue would thus be directed away from the Forest Department's general purpose coffers (where it could be used anywhere). It would belong entirely to the MPFDC and could be reinvested in Bastar and, eventually, in other industrial projects.

The corporation was to become a vehicle to encourage further loans, having built up equity in the project. In a simpler, physical sense, an improved network of roads and communication would link the plantations—roads more capable of carrying big timber trucks than the present narrow roads. The rest of the district's infrastructure would remain intact. The cost of the new roads would be borne by sale of the existing forest. In short, an asset under control of an old government department more inclined to conservation, would be stripped and replaced with something of unknown value, under control of a new government corporation with an orientation to rapid industrial extraction.

The old department had had a reputation for expertise in botany, silviculture, soil analysis, entomology, and for enforcing the conservation codes and laws of the forest. The new corporation was to be staffed by a new kind of specialist with expertise in logistics, engineering, management, and marketing. These different orientations were revealed in small ways; for example, the new corporation mapped "catchment areas" for forestry studies. These areas were discontinuous with the old "ranges", which had been administered and patrolled (in paramilitary fashion) by the Forest Department. Again, as a sign of the old department's sense of its own priority, these ranges had been laid out to be discontinuous with the basic tehsils into which this district, like others, was divided by other departments for purposes such as revenue or tribal welfare.

In summary, the TAP initiated processes leading to changes in these three environments: the biological, the social, and the legal-administrative. No large-scale migration occurred into Bastar as a specific part of the TAP project, and few tribals were engaged in the project in any prolonged, significant way. This lack of involvement, in itself, is the striking feature of the natural history of the project.

CHAPTER 5

The Project and the Tribal Study

People are not convinced the project is going to be a permanent one.
—Tribal Research and Development Institute, 1980

AS IN other World Bank projects, an oral history ran parallel to the documented history of the Bastar project. We are not presenting a case study of the project-cycle of the Bank. In fact, some of the components of a complete and balanced history of the Bastar project will not be obtainable for a number of years.[1] But the evolution of the project has been observed, read, and discussed. It can be roughly outlined here.

The Natural History of the Project

In May 1975 a World Bank mission to Bastar concluded that the project should proceed. Within two months the state's forestry development corporation was created—the new vehicle for the project and for a new kind of forestry. In October 1975 technical assistance to India's forestry was recommended to the Bank's executive directors, and two months later the Bastar project proposal was approved. Although this rapid activity culminated years of plodding study and proposals, by Indian standards the pace was dizzying. Cash flowed into the project offices in April 1976, and serious forestry studies started in 1977.

At the beginning of 1978 a public-relations booklet, released by the MPFDC, repeated the idea of "complementary schemes" to create employment opportunities for tribals by controlled management in the nistari forests, thus preserving the other forests for exclusive MPFDC use. That phrase, in fact, had been lifted from the original loan document. This time, however, a prediction was given for employment:

"More than a million job opportunities were expected to be created with execution of this project."[2] Photographs showed researchers interviewing women and children in tribal villages, though the tribal study had not even been planned at that stage. Japanese (Komatsu) bulldozers were shown smashing down trees and tearing stumps out of the ground, and workers were shown cutting logs into movable lengths with chain saws. Full-time employment would be achieved because an all-weather paved road was planned, allowing logging in the rainy season. Not shown were the apartments being constructed for corporation officers in Jagdalpur, the corporation's office compound with jeeps and cars, and two enormous yellow Swedish (Volvo) log loaders sitting inactive in the yard.

Meanwhile the MPFDC discovered that single-crop plantations were proving vulnerable to insect attack. Just north of Bastar, the corporation carried out aerial spraying of young teak plantations in 1978 to try to stop defoliation by insects.[3] Using malathion, carbaryl, and fenitortion, the corporation reported that it achieved 84–99.6 percent kill rates—but it did not report the results of its studies of effects on wildlife and the natural predators of the defoliating pests, nor did it report the costs of such measures. With Caribbean pine (hondurensis), the MPFDC would eventually face *Fomes annosus*, a fungus that had caused 37 percent losses in Jamaican pine plantations.[4] This fungus is endemic in practically every forest, plantation, and stand of trees worldwide. The project's planning had included little analysis of vulnerability to pests and diseases on the Bastar pine plantations.

At the end of 1978 the TAP had to face some very hard facts. The size of the pulp mill originally planned would require cutting trees from 4,600 hectares (1 hectare: 2.47 acres). Yet the MPFDC now conceded that 2,000 hectares would be their upper limit—eventually. At that time they were clearing about one hundred hectares per year. Anyone who has stood in the middle of one hundred clear-cut hectares in a forest knows its vast size. The approach to the Caribbean pine was then only at the research stage in Bastar; thinning and pruning studies were in progress. But the real worry was whether the pine tree would succeed in the full-scale plantation environment. International experts had already expressed their doubts at meetings in 1978. Among such experts, data on bamboo were considered "hopeless," because at that stage it was not known whether there would be enough bamboo to feed the mill. Quite apart from these issues, however, the study of impact of the whole investment on tribal life had simply not begun.

Although the five-year World Bank loan was to be used to determine whether the intensive forestry project was feasible, by 1978–1979 there was a definite expectation in some quarters that the project would obtain a major commitment (hence, the capital construction). With respect to private investment, however, which had already been mentioned in other documents, the MPFDC report said all the studies done in the previous ten years had tempted private investors and industrialists, but still they had not been "converted to action." In fact, their caution was based on the same unresolved project issues that also helped to stop the World Bank's investment:

> The major hesitation on the part of industrialists to invest large sums of money in pulp and paper industry was due to certain questions like resource base, size and configuration of pulp/paper mills, markets, the logistics of harvesting large volumes of timber, species and provenance trials and the technical basis for establishment of large scale pine and other fast growing species.[5]

By early 1979 the timber and soil resources had been estimated, the water fluctuations in Bastar's rivers had been measured, and the domestic pulp and paper consumption as well as the export potential had all been forecast. This work was jointly done by Development Consultants Ltd. of Calcutta and by Sandwell Management Consultants Ltd. of Vancouver. The Calcutta engineering firm had retained a retired head of the Indian Forest Department (the Inspector General of Forests) and had provided him with a small plane for flying to Bastar. Presumably one of his functions was to smooth feelings among the foresters and the state department with respect to the creation of the new corporation. The Vancouver forestry firm had done studies of this kind in many countries, often for the World Bank, and was familiar with the Indian administrative and commercial conditions.

At first the TAP team thought it might house itself in the palace complex of the late Maharajah of Bastar, but eventually it settled for a modern house in Jagdalpur. During this year, hardwoods from Bastar were made into pulp for paper-making in order to test for brightness, strength, and pulpability. Using wood from trees of diameters between 11 and 50 centimeters, the study concluded that bleachable grade pulps in acceptable yields could be made from Bastar mixed hardwoods.[6] Experts came and went: some pored over red satellite photographs of the forest cover, others walked miles through the forest counting species of trees. Much effort was given to this empirical work, with a regular checking and consultation on results, including meetings with Bank officials and government officials. Cooperation, or at least consultation, was evident on all sides.

The final report by Sandwell, presented in 1979, proposed a pine-plantation-based pulp and paper mill in Bastar to produce 100,000 finished tons per annum. Foreign exchange savings were forecast at between $1.2 billion and $700 million within twenty-five years. While the report spoke about possible adverse effects upon tribal life of the project, the model on which it was planned did not have the benefit of any empirical studies on the relation of the project to tribal life. The Sandwell report referred cryptically to meetings with those in Bhopal who would probably carry out such studies: "The Tribal Study Group (of the state government) indicated during discussions in Bhopal that they do not see any insurmountable problems."[7] Nevertheless, the report dwelt at length on the risks from industrial forestry to tribal subsistence patterns. Thus, said the report, tribals must be motivated to accept change in forest practices, and nontribal people must be educated to grasp the problems faced by tribals "in order to reduce incidence of tribal exploitation and antagonism." "Social change planned in a systematic fashion is preferable for all concerned, wherever possible."[8] All of the feasibility study's focus was on minimizing adverse social effects. At that stage (September 1979) no study of the tribal-forest relationship had been conducted as part of the project.

Amongst all this other work, a key provision of the Bank's 1975 project document was a study on tribals (see table 1) to determine "the impact on tribal life of large-scale forest industrial development from 1980 onwards."[9] Estimated to require one hundred man-months, the study was to be carried out by an interdepartmental study team established by the state of Madhya Pradesh, monitored by a full-time sociologist and social anthropologist, and coordinated with the industrial feasibility studies through a committee specially created for the purpose. Although the duration of the feasibililty study was planned for twenty months (and it took longer), the duration of the study on tribals was planned for six months (and it took less time than that). The

Bank's consultants were to monitor the whole process and to integrate results of the tribal study with their recommendations. Apparently no foreign exchange was set aside for this purpose in the agreement, but about 2.5 percent of the Indian contribution of $4 million (i.e., $100,000) was assigned to the tribal study. Of even lower priority was the "environmental study," planned with a month in the field and a month in the home office. It must be remembered that the agencies charged with tribal welfare and tribal development were of low status when compared with the Forestry Department and the corporation. Communication between the tribal agency and its field officers was (in the late 1970s) very poor. Multiline telephones installed in its district headquarters permitted calls within the building, but not to the field, and rarely to Bhopal. They were merely props in the ritual display of bureaucratic life, purchased in one of the waves of financing "tribal uplift."

Until this time, most recent publications on the sociology and anthropology of Bastar were based on empirical research done between 1958 and 1960, under "the Bastar project" of the Anthropological Survey of India.[10] Although useful in some ways, this corpus of work did not add much to knowledge of the relation of people and trees in Bastar. When the World Bank loaned $4 million and the Government of India matched this sum for the TAP, they offered, in effect, the first significant means in twenty years to create publicly accessible, carefully gathered longitudinal data on the relation of people, trees, and land. And yet little of lasting value seems to have come from this $8 million opportunity.

In fact, nothing was done about the tribal study for three years following the agreement. Two years into the project, it was reported that the tribal question had not even been discussed, and the MPFDC had shown no interest in the topic. At a 1978 review meeting in Delhi, the tribal question was raised once, and there was brief discussion of adjusting the size and location of the pulp mill to suit the vulnerable nature of tribal life.[11] Up to that point, the only recent information was in two studies, in 1975 and 1977, on the social and economic life of the tribals, and on social forestry in Bastar. In connection with his other work (but only incidental to it), forester V. G. Kohli of the central government surveyed 341 households in forty-six villages between December 1975 and June 1977. From his own estimates, he concluded that earlier calculations on the rate of extraction of small timber, bamboo, firewood, and thatching grass by tribals were much too low, perhaps by 33 to 50 percent. Kohli found tribal dependence on the forests, therefore, to be greater than had been recognized, affecting their diet as well as their housing and fuel—not to speak of their spiritual life.[12]

The exploitation of tribals by outsiders, Kohli had advised, could be stopped only if economic progress were made "without undermining the tribals' heritage and without disrupting their way of life." And social forestry, he argued, would be "a step in the right direction"; the nistari forests, also called the orange areas, would have to be scientifically managed and made productive by controlling bamboo and tree growth, and by adding new income-bearing trees—like fruit trees—in the presently overexploited tribal areas.[13] Although it was a popular concept in international thinking at the time, and although the Bank was promoting the concept elsewhere, social forestry did not play a central role in the planning of the Bastar project or the proposed operation of the MPFDC.[14]

During 1977 a Madhya Pradesh parliamentary committee on the welfare of scheduled castes and scheduled tribes visited Bastar to meet with local officials and discuss the future of the forests. They investigated the extent of exploitation of tribals in the purchase of forest products and payment for their labor. The negative effects of the Bailadila iron ore mine (to be discussed below) and its use of migrant labor instead of the tribal workers were discussed. The indefinite nature of tribal occupation of land or trees, and the consequent alienation of land by legal and illegal means, were contrasted with problems of getting adequate disbursement of subsidies and grants to offset the economic displacement of tribals. All of this was discussed before the Bailadila massacre in 1978, and before most of the clear-cutting for the pine plantations. Combined with the critical conclusions of the 1980 Tribal Research and Development Institute study, this committee's investigation probably provided the grounds for some of the opposition to the continuation of the project.[15] In particular, the committee warned against the rapid curtailment of nistari rights for tribals in the forests, because the alternatives of social forestry were evidently a long way off in Bastar. This was not consistent with the recommendations of the National Commission on Agriculture regarding the eventual abolition of nistari rights, and their replacement with social forestry, as we shall show below.

Finally, in 1979, the Tribal Research and Development Institute in Bhopal was instructed to prepare and carry out a tribal study. The institute obtained the approval of its research plan from a Bank supervisory mission, both in terms of selected objectives and scientific design.[16] In the Kurundi area, where the first impact of the industrial forestry was expected to be greatest, 1,700 households in twenty villages (out of a total of fifty-eight available villages) would be surveyed. If successful, this survey would later be extended to cover the entire project area. But the results of this study by the Tribal Research and Development Institute, when submitted to the state government, were not circulated. "We have unofficially learned that a report was submitted to the government of Madhya Pradesh, but it has not been released," wrote a World Bank official.[17] The Canadian firm conducting the other studies in Bastar stated in 1980 and 1981 that it had not received any tribal-study report. A Bank official said that the Madhya Pradesh government did not find the report in line with the given terms of reference. An Indian newspaper account in October 1981 said the institute's 1979 study had demonstrated that, in the long run, the forestry project would adversely affect the lives of the tribals and would cripple their economy, dependent upon the sal forests. The sal tree was needed for the pulp mills until the pine plantations would be ready for use in fifteen years.[18]

The uncirculated study was only half the scale of the one originally planned. It led to definitely negative conclusions about the pine plantations from the tribal perspective. Nevertheless, according to an FAO mission, "The Indian authorities and the Bank decided in 1980 that a point had been reached where an investment project could be formulated."[19] So while these investment plans were being made, a report critical of the project lay in the state capitol offices. Officials of other departments (e.g., tribal welfare) were now capable of lobbying against the project as much as some foresters were lobbying for it. Late in 1980 the FAO dispatched a mission to Bastar, at the Bank's request, in order to examine sawmilling, pulp and paper, plantation, and fire control in the project as well as its relation to tribal society. On arrival, this mission learned that the project concept "had become politically contentious due to tribal issues" concerned mainly with the clearing of native sal for pine plantations and with the adverse effects of industrial forestry.[20] By the time the FAO mission submitted its report in the spring of 1981, a subcommittee of the Madhya Pradesh cabinet had already recommended approval of the project subject to safeguards for tribals, but this had not been given approval by the full state cabinet. At this time there were eleven Bastar members of the legislature of Madhya Pradesh: one nontribal member from the town of Jagdalpur and ten reserved seats held by tribals in other parts of the district. The Bank and Indian government officials in favor of the project had obviously seen impending difficulties and had obtained approval for a one-year extension of the TAP to allow time for political approval and the arrival of a favorable FAO report. This report, which included some criticisms but presented a means of saving the project in a scaled-down version, appeared just before the World Bank made its own reappraisal mission in the spring of 1981.

By October 1981, however, the Government of India announced it would review the entire matter. Criticism of the project was voiced by biologists and ecologists at a symposium on tropical ecology in Bhopal. According to a press report, the government sanctioned a Rs 600,000 research grant to Rewa University in Madhya Pradesh to "take a fresh look at the pine plantation project."[21] After the expiry of the TAP, a Bank official wrote that "GoI has finally reviewed the project. Its findings have not yet been officially sent to us but informally we have heard that they are against the project."[22] A year later an official wrote that the Government of India had decided to retain the present current forest management system for Bastar.

The Conclusions of the Tribal Study

In essence, the 1980 draft report on tribals presented, at times laconically and at times passionately, most of the criticisms of the TAP which had already been made orally. But it did so from a tribal perspective. If it was indeed based largely upon the views of affected tribal people, this shows how congruent were the perceptions of tribals and the local nontribal elite who had already voiced opinions. If it was not, and if a tribal perspective was merely a vehicle for opinions of an elite, this shows how a segment of the population not directly affected by the project nevertheless opposed it. What follows is an outline of the study's scope and conclusions; its observations of conditions within the TAP are particularly valuable.

The study selected ten villages from among forty-nine in Jagdalpur tehsil from which laborers had already come to work on the pine project. All villages fell within forty-seven kilometers of the three different project work sites. Just as one-fifth of the villages were selected, so were one-fifth (492) of the households within them. Each village had a primary school, and four had middle schools. Nine of the villages had drinking-water wells. Although two had veterinary dispensaries for livestock, none had medical facilities for their people. They were populated by a representative range of scheduled tribes and castes, each with different rates of literacy and education. Each of the villages was close to Jagdalpur, so the data reflected the results of tribal employment in addition to the minor investments made by the state. "The conclusions of this report, therefore, [had] extreme limitations for applicability to Bastar as a whole."[23] Nevertheless, the study described social conditions in the project zone of impact in 1980. It is the only record of an official attempt to do so.

The report states that 75 percent of the sample population of 9,300 people (between the ages of 15 and 60) expressed no interest in working for the pine project. A majority of these also expressed some antipathy toward the development of the project so far. Among the 25 percent interested in working, some were already working primarily in forestry. Among those not interested in working, forestry was already a subsidiary occupation. The economic reliance upon the forests was high—at dependence level in more than half the households for certain key items. So disinterest in or indifference to the project, and even opposition to it, was based on considerable knowledge. The report offers possible causes for this negative opinion in these 492 households, which are listed here without assigning priority to any. (Page numbers refer to the report itself.)

1. Wage earning was generally looked down upon by most tribals because it was associated with excessive organization. The tribals had "an independent nature" (p. 76), so their attitude was one of being "not serious" about work. The industrial scale did not suit them.

2. Different work was evaluated differently: felling trees with a chain saw was risky and exhausting, planting pines was work for women and children; timber-depot work provided slightly higher status and was for adult men only, and so on. New tasks were already

classified in terms of the existing labor market. Some tasks were thought to be insufficiently paid, and so people pursued alternatives less strenuous, less dangerous, or less distant from home. There was a general dislike of working "like a coolie" outside one's own village area.

3. Although laborers were supposed to be provided with transport to and from work, the TAP vehicles did not always arrive. The people were told to travel by public bus. They were not always reimbursed; also they lost time for which they were not paid.

4. Payment was not always made before the weekend or on promised days, and it was sometimes only partial. Sometimes the balance was paid in wheat, not cash; wheat was not a preferred food for tribals (and may have been associated in their minds with relief regulations). These practices, over the months, made people suspicious of the TAP and some of its front-line staff.

5. In the logging area there was seldom any drinking water provided and little first aid for accidents. No huts were constructed for the workers' temporary use.

6. A sudden accidental death at the logging site caused tribals to withdraw completely. Their "superstitious" responses in other instances were ridiculed by corporation staff but, the report states, "Bastar tribals are known for deserting villages and settling elsewhere on this account" (p. 113).

7. A contractor from the adjacent state was awarded the right to make charcoal from project waste wood at Kurundi. He did not employ tribals even for petty jobs. Nevertheless, the air of the village was regularly polluted with smoke.

8. In Kurundi village the water tank, focus of social life, bathing and laundry, had been drawn down, without compensation, because water was pumped out for the project.

9. Other casual labor was available closer—the Public Works Department (PWD) stone quarry, and regular Forest Department work—so people could reach home in the evening (especially women). On TAP work, they often ended up sleeping on site because of the high cost of transportation, for which they did not expect to get reimbursed.

10. Work targets and rates were fixed arbitrarily by different supervisors. Some staff were disliked, others appreciated. Tribal people were

fine calculators of the comparative disadvantage of piece rates or daily rates for wages, given the kind of task.

11. People saw by example that pine was very vulnerable to fire in the hot season, and they knew that preparations to fight fires in the existing plantations—not to mention the proposed plantation surrounding more valuable forest—were totally inadequate.

12. Ten years earlier nearby protected forests had been clear-cut as part of the usual forest management. This had forced adjacent villagers to walk 8-10 kilometers to obtain firewood and minor forest products for their daily use. So now that 1,500 hectares of the Kangar reserved forest were already clear-cut for pine plantations, "this has shocked the villagers and they find it difficult to get fuel and minor forest products" (p. 86). "It is the feeling of the people, confirmed by observations in the field, that in future this distance is going to be increased if the pace of felling continues" (p. 66).

13. While livestock were grazing in the forest, people would collect firewood, or seeds, or flowers. Now there is nowhere to graze and nothing to collect unless one goes far from home. Of course some forest products might be purchased at the depot of the Forest Department: "The things that people used to get free from the forest have now to be purchased. The very idea is shocking to the people and they are left bewildered" (p. 67). They jest that even for a twig to clean their teeth, they are handicapped.

Project officials evidently tried to counteract some of this feeling with what the report called "welfare programmes" at the nursery and plantation work sites. A fair price store was established to sell consumer goods (rice, soap, vegetables, eggs, honey, etc.). Two tribals took loans to start their own poultry farms, eggs from which were purchased by the project. Veterinarians were sent to visit these farms. A trained beekeeper established a honey project for twenty households, but it was not successful—one reason given was that smoke from the nearby charcoal project drove away the bees. Four rope-making machines, which used fibers from the local mesta plant, were bought to allow villagers to make their own rope. Finally, adult education classes were offered during the lunch hour.

Strong precedence underlies the skeptical attitude of tribals to plantations of new species touted as valuable to their lives. In 1962, before

Caribbean pine was first tentatively planted in Bastar, 6,600 hectares of eucalyptus plantations were introduced—some into forest clear-cut by the department. The eucalyptus tree has subsequently been described as an "ecological terrorist"—it is good only for paper mills and synthetic rayon mills, and it provides almost no fuel, fodder, green mulch, or shade. In addition, its growing and thirsty physiology lowers the water table. Yet, when introduced, these plantations were described as potentially beneficial to the tribals.

In the tribal view this useless experiment foreshadowed the pine project fifteen years later. Yet the dilemma of the relation between the official terms "social forestry" and "production forestry" continued to press itself upon the political hierarchy. After the Bastar project began, the Madhya Pradesh Minister of Forests (who was also Minister of Panchayat and Social Welfare, and Community Development) said that because modern scientific forestry schemes generate employment potential and create infrastructure, "they ultimately benefit the weaker sections of the people in remote tribal tracts."[24] At the same time, Chief Minister S. C. Shukla, said:

> A new concept of social forestry, called "Panch Vans," has been introduced so that viable forests are created outside the normal reserved forests in order to meet the nistari rights of the population. These "Panch Vans" are being created by the Forest Department with the help of the villagers, and the standard of development being applied is no less than that prevailing in a reserved forest. Ten years from now Madhya Pradesh can look forward to increasing its forest area by at least 80,000 hectares by way of "Panch Vans." This, then, would be the only State in the country which will have created from scratch forests which belong to the people, are managed by them, and [are] reserved exclusively to meet their needs. [25]

Noble as these forestry schemes sound, they are not based on the experiences of the past: this is not so much due to willful avoidance as to the fact that the experiences of the past have been buried—even those which have been successful. Understandably, a Minister of Forests or a Chief Minister would seldom learn these lessons. And, just as understandably, people living in Bastar forests would be very skeptical. But the idea of forests for tribal use and control keeps reappearing. At the beginning of the pine project, thoughtful proposals from V. G. Kohli, a senior forester in Bastar, were found exciting by many people interested in the project. Kohli pointed out the large amount of land available in 1976 for "social forestry": 4,800 square kilometers of orange area (forest left outside the demarcated protected forest areas) and 5,700 square kilometers wasteland within village boundaries (village "banjer").[26] This potential land was separate from the 21,700 square kilometers directly controlled by the Forest Department. Kohli's main contribution was to establish that the estimates of the National Commission on Agriculture regarding the tribal economic dependence on forests were, in Bastar, about half of what was actually the case. The official rate of extraction was thus a gross underestimate if applied to Bastar. His plans tried to account for this fact. In 1981 the FAO mission predicated its recommendation for a pulp mill and pine plantations on realistic proposals for very large and well-managed "social forestry" schemes involving fruit orchards. How these schemes were to engage the tribal people was, as usual, the unknown factor. Each advocate recognized that the lead time required to "get started" was much longer than in the case of industrial forestry.

It is important to see the situation in Bastar comparatively; other tribal areas of India have experienced more profound upheavals, including confrontations with military forces. The sense of *relative* opportunity in Bastar for new forest-tribe-government relations was borne out by many experienced observers. Some options seemed to remain open; not everything was closed with sabers drawn. The dean of foreign observers of the tribal situation in India, C. von Furer-Haimendorf, sensed this during a jeep journey through Bastar in the late 1970s: he visited Gond villages and weekly markets, traveled to the remote Abujhmar Hills, and spoke to tribals and officials. The good situation there, he said, could be credited to efforts of enlightened and liberal civil administration to control the exploitative relations of tribal and nontribal people in Bastar. Thus, the "tribal people lead a life in accordance with their own traditions and inclinations."[27] This optimism contrasted strongly with the foreboding he felt about the pine project, as we shall see.

Beyond the causes listed above and the responses made by the corporation, the tribal study concluded that the overall tribal reasoning followed a more profound logic. "Forests are so interwoven with the tribal life that it is beyond the imagination of a tribal to survive without forests, because of the ecological setting of a tribal village, socio-religious equilibrium, and economic dependence" (p. 107). "The tribals' psychological as well as economic dependence on forests is paramount and is reflected in all walks of their life" (p. 5). "Now that the forests in the area are being cut and the tribals' rights in the forests have been curtailed, the tribal is apprehensive and suspicious" (p. 108). A valued species is being replaced by something without value. Tribals point out that the pattern repeats the history of the first plantation of eucalyptus in Bastar, in which "a vague hope was given that it [would] yield oil, employment, etc. What the villagers found was deprivation on a massive scale with an alien species without any relevance to the local economy" (pp. 4, 5). What the project offered was wage labor, but "the concept of wage labor will not satisfy the tribal and will always bring him in confrontation with the new economic system" (p. 9). "The tribal owns land and has a right over forests. The moment this relationship is converted into money which he cannot handle, he is at the mercy of a system which he does not know" (p. 7). Perception of the pine project was based on the tribals' understanding of tribal and nontribal relations in Bastar. The corporation did not come to buy or steal their land. "The fact, however, is that the tribes who owned all the land are now becoming landless and the immigrants are becoming landed" (p. 47). The corporation and project shared a natural alignment with other outside forces and formed the vanguard for some of them. "It is an irony that the Corporation itself has acquired an identity the welfare of whose members becomes a high priority and central to the entire scheme of things" (pp. 9, 10). "The situation stands further aggravated by the fact that the regulatory functions of the Forest Department being hitherto exercised by Forest officials working for the management of the forests are now being exercised by the officials of the Corporation, which is purely a commercial organization concerned with the economic exploitation of the forests" (p. 11). The corporation had only one staff member in 1980 who could speak the Gondi language. Further, the report charged that the corporation lacked understanding of psychological factors of tribal work and tribal life. Most profound of all, however, was a realization voiced by the tribals regarding the whole undertaking: "People are not convinced that the project is going to be a permanent one" (p. 110). And the tribals were right.

CHAPTER 6

Market Trends, Alternative Investments, Unresolved Issues

The decision to convert this sal forest to industrially more valuable species like teak may satisfy the needs for higher revenues which may or may not be used for the welfare of these same people, but would certainly deprive them of an output from the forest which they are enjoying. —Inspector General of Forests, India, 1981

IN 1981 the Bastar pine plantation was terminated. Given the history of great expectations for a major forestry project in Bastar, why was this particular project stopped? We cannot give a definite answer, but we can offer some contending possibilities. We would suggest the following explanations, listed in rough inverse order of apparent importance: fluctuation of world pulp and paper prices; options for alternate pulp and paper investment in India; and unresolved project issues and divided opinion.

Fluctuation of World Pulp and Paper Prices

From 1980 the prices of both newsprint and bleached pulp dropped considerably on world markets. Estimates based on price trends made in 1978–1979, particularly those for the Sandwell and Company report, could not hold. The idea of a "world price" is itself a guideline without official status, but it is widely communicated throughout the industry and is adjusted on a quarterly basis. Variations from the world price include the spot market, in which prices may be as much as 50 percent higher than the world price, and long-term contracts (adjusted quarterly), in which the world price is discounted.

Apart from such variations, the record shows wide price fluctuations for hardwood bleached kraft pulp and newsprint during the life of the Bastar forestry project. Pulp prices, at a prevailing high just before the project commenced, dropped during 1976 to a marked low in late 1977.

Prices then climbed steadily from late 1978 until early 1980. They remained steady for almost two years, during which time planners were deciding whether to continue the project. Following 1981, pulp prices experienced a drop to the levels of 1977(see table 4). It should be

TABLE 4
Pulp and Newsprint Price Fluctuation, 1976–1981
(Current US dollars per ton)

	Hardwood Bleached Kraft Pulp US Delivery		Newsprint Eastern US Delivery	
	Highest	Lowest	Highest	Lowest
1976	335	320	300	260
1977	290	220	305	300
1978	300	250	320	305
1979	380	340	375	320
1980	445	395	400	375
1981	435	430	500	470

Source: The Paper Trade Journal (1976–1982).

noted that these figures, based on public data, do not reflect the common practice of discounting, which has resulted in a secular decline of prices. Discounted values, often up to 33 percent, are not publicly disclosed.[1] The newsprint prices, conversely, rose steadily throughout the entire period (in current dollars). Looked at in terms of constant dollars, however, the prices in 1980 and 1981 represent a plateau and decline. This would suggest two downturns in newsprint price trends during the project period.

India was importing about 300,000 tons of newsprint before the project. Most of the production from Bastar was to be sold in the domestic market. Nonetheless, planners would have seen that even protected domestic markets might not sustain new costs of production and uncertain supply of raw materials in India against underutilized capacity and low paper and pulp prices from abroad. There was considerable dumping of southern U.S. hardwood pulp during these downturns, particularly in Asian markets. The desire for import substitution in newsprint in India had to be weighed against the economics of the world market, and the microeconomics of individual mills in India.

In addition, some Indian newspaper publishers were known to oppose further newspulp and paper production capacity in the country because they were convinced that, if they did not own the productive industry, they would be hostage to protected domestic prices. They would thus lose the advantage of international price fluctuations.

Options for Alternate Pulp and Paper Investment in India

The pulp and paper mill in Bastar was intended to deal with India's newsprint situation. When the World Bank project began, India's capacity to produce newsprint did not exceed 75,000 tons per year. In 1974 India produced 48,500 tons; in 1975, 52,000 tons; and in 1978, 55,500 tons. The actual use of newsprint, however, was much greater—so in 1974–1975 the cost of importing about 300,000 tons of newsprint was Rs 195.6 million, paid, of course, in foreign exchange. In 1973 the whole bamboo market was nationalized, and existing leases for bamboo pulp plantations were terminated. Illicit cutting was presumed stopped, and fresh leases were established at new rates: five pulp and paper mills in Madhya Pradesh continued to operate, but the planned Bastar mill was expected to process 100,000 to 250,000 tons of pulp per year.

India had become the world's tenth largest importer of newsprint by 1980, at 140,000 tons, and the ninth largest producer of printing and writing paper—producing 2.7 percent of the world total, slightly more than the USSR. On the consumption scale, India was eighth in the world as consumer of printing and writing paper in 1980, with 2.8 percent of the world total, but was not among the top ten consumers of newsprint. India was also tenth in the world among consumers of hardwood in 1980.[2] In an effort to identify developing countries as emerging trading partners, Bethel and Tseng provided data through which to assess the position of specific countries in 1982, with respect to eighty-eight other middle-income countries (like Jamaica), low-income countries (like India), and least-developed countries (like Haiti). India ranked high in these data, which listed the top ten developing countries: in wood pulp consumption, India ranked fifth largest; in wood pulp imports, sixth

TABLE 5

Trade in Wood Pulp and Newsprint, 1982

Woodpulp Consumption	% of top ten	Thousand metric tons
Brazil	30.8	2,119
Indonesia	17.3	1,188
Mexico	9.8	671
South Korea	9.7	670
India	8.6	591
Argentina	6.2	424

Woodpulp Imports	% of top ten	Thousand metric tons
South Korea	23.7	435
Mexico	11.7	214
Venezuela	9.4	173
Argentina	8.1	148
Indonesia	6.4	118
India	5.9	108
Thailand	4.9	90

Newsprint Consumption	% of top ten	Thousand metric tons
Mexico	15.8	476
Brazil	10.3	311
India	9.2	278
South Korea	7.6	229
Turkey	5.2	157

Newsprint Imports	% of top ten	Thousand metric tons
Mexico	17.5	351
India	11.6	232
Brazil	10.3	206
Venezuela	7.0	140
El Salvador	6.5	130

Source: Adapted from data on 88 countries (to display status of India) from James Bethel and Adelina Y. Tseng, "Developing Countries as Markets for Forest Products," in *World Trade in Forest Products*, Gerald F. Schreuder, ed. (Seattle: University of Washington Press, 1986), pp. 11–47.

largest; in newsprint consumption and imports, third and second respectively (see table 5).[3] Clearly the Bastar project was intended to meet a need that had not diminished by 1982, and decline in demand was not a reason for terminating the project.

The Bastar project was not the only pulp and paper investment being considered by the World Bank in India. Even while its officials were trying to get the Bastar proposal approved in Bhopal and New Delhi, albeit in a scaled-down version of the earlier plans, another candidate project was in the wings. In mid-September 1981, a $100 million loan was announced by the World Bank for a pulp and paper mill in southern India—Tamil Nadu. Using available bagasse from five nearby sugar mills, mixed with about 20 percent eucalyptus fiber, the mill would produce newsprint as well as paper for printing and writing. Designed by an American-British consortium, to be implemented by it along with local companies, the project would have an additional $137.5 million contributed by the state government and the private sector. As the news release announced, "This will be the first project in the pulp and paper industry to be financed by the World Bank in India."[4] Terms were 10.6 percent interest per year for twenty years, including five years' grace. This mill began to operate in 1985.

World Bank planners were under a special pressure during the Bastar project. Until 1978 loans in the forestry sector had been infrequent and on an ad hoc basis, but in 1978 a decision was made to loan $800 million between 1978 and 1983, a four-fold increase over the 1972–1976 period. Of this total, $300 million was already earmarked for pulp and paper projects, and for the remaining $500 million, twenty-five projects were, like Bastar, already in preparation.[5] In fiscal 1979 the Bank invested $178.7 million in forestry and related projects (compared with $74.0 million in 1976), bringing its historic total to $1.166 billion ($852 million for commercial forestry projects and $314 million for other forestry assistance).[6] In 1980 a proposal was made in the energy sector policy paper to increase the Bank's loans to fuelwood projects to $1 billion between 1981 and 1985. The pressure to commit and disperse funds, spoken of by Bank officials, was very real indeed. This suggests why great efforts were made to avoid the termination of the Bastar project.

In the same 1981 announcement (the Tamil Nadu loan), as if to comfort the government of Madhya Pradesh, the World Bank announced an International Development Association (IDA) credit worth $220 million (to be matched by state funds) for irrigation systems to take advantage of the major Mahanadi and Hasdeo Bango projects. The IDA credit, in the form of special drawing rights, was for fifty years, with ten years' grace, at no interest but a 0.75 percent service charge. Not only would the government's Irrigation Department be able to expand dramatically, but private contractors would also be able to bid competitively for $151 million worth of small construction work that would directly benefit the private sector.

There had been clear expectations at the start of the project that the private sector would invest in Bastar. The 1975 World Bank proposals for technical assistance in forestry said that the Baroda Rayon Corporation planned a $70 million rayon-grade pulp mill, and Bangur Brothers planned a $110 million veneer and plywood mill. Although the Bank and the Government of India looked forward to these investments, to utilize the cutting capacity of the MPFDC, the preliminary evidence suggested difficulties: the annual wood requirement (excluding bamboo) of these two projects was 900,000 cubic meters. This required an estimated clear-cutting of 18,000 hectares or 180 square kilometers every year. Within a short time, Bangur Brothers thought their plywood mill would better be located out of Bastar, but the rayon mill remained a distinct hope. In addition, the Bank said in 1975 that plans for a large steel mill were being studied in Bastar (by unnamed investors). Obviously the conjunction of iron ore and hydroelectric power was attractive, but steel-making requires a lot of water. Were the steel mill to proceed, it would adversely affect the water available for a pulp and paper mill. By 1980–1981 it appeared that none of these private investments would be implemented. Protagonists of the Bastar project would have to accept the fact that the government would be working alone.

Not only were the institutional arrangements in the Tamil Nadu project more attractive, given the new mood in the Bank toward private-sector involvement (Ronald Reagan had been elected president of the United States, and a new World Bank president, A. W. Clausen, had been chosen from within the private American banking community), but also the serious environmental and sociological concerns in the Bastar project were avoided. After all, the Bank had already expressed itself on environmental and social consequences of deforestation in its 1978 forestry sector policy paper: "Securing the co-operation of local people who are destroying the forests creates formidable social problems. . . . Methods to ameliorate the abuses . . . can be both costly and politically unpopular."[7] The policy paper also underlined "the weakness of forestry institutions" as "perhaps the single most important obstacle in increasing forestry activity by the Bank."[8] Firewood, deforestation, and the social impact of forest industries had also become fashionable questions in Washington, D.C., by this time, and a number of United States government agencies were being asked about their policies and practices bearing upon deforestation in developing countries.[9] Finally, a number of pulp mills operating in India were like the one planned for Bastar (100,000 tons). These were well known to be uncompetitive and marginally profitable, or even unprofitable. Combined with the other technical problems, this fact constituted an obstacle. At the same time, the idea was circulated in Bastar that a large paper mill in neighboring Maharashtra state, operated by the huge Birla Corporation, already was treating southwestern Bastar as its catchment area for its bamboo needs. Any project in Bastar, it was said, would interfere with the needs of the Birla mill. Interfering with a company of such power would be fatal to the Bastar project, if it went ahead, argued informed people in Jagdalpur. This increase in the "ambient level of concern" would have reached some officials in the Bank as well as the Government of India, encouraging them to question further the Bastar project.

Unresolved Project Issues and Divided Opinion

It is known that government officials in Bastar were not uniformly favorable to the TAP; their opinions seem to have been as divided as among the public at large. Although a cabinet subcommittee had recommended its continuation, a government department's report had blasted it. Public criticism must have had its effects within the government. Eventually, we believe, there were confrontations involving various ministries, including the Forest Departments at state and central levels. In addition to the interaction of the district's interest groups, which were going to be positively and negatively affected by the pulp and paper investment, there remained a number of unresolved "technical" issues, even as late as spring 1981. There were four basic issues of concern: the supply of wood; the classification of the forest land and resources; the status of tribals in that classification; and the capabilities of the forestry development corporation.

Wood Supply. The 1981 FAO mission's report raised doubts that in the soils of Bastar the Caribbean pine would grow to optimum height. Detailed soil surveys were not conducted during the entire project period. Small-scale tests in Bastar had yielded poor results; tests elsewhere in India were also small-scale. The investment, therefore, would have to rely on research done in other countries, in so-called homoclimes. Expert conclusion from such results, however, had not been uniform, and the problem of site-specificity had overpowered the value of extrapolation from homoclime research. In addition, a reported worldwide shortage of Caribbean pine seeds suitable for industrial purposes was reported. Nurseries in Bastar had, after initial success, performed poorly according to the FAO mission.

The first Caribbean pines (*P. caribaea*) were planted in Bastar in 1968, and again in 1972: when Saxena reported on their growth in 1976, the average diameter after eight years was 8.0 centimeters. The survival rate of *P. caribaea (hondurensis)* was 96 percent, and of *P. caribaea (caribaea)*, 76 percent after eight years.[10] The introduction of Caribbean pine to Bastar was stopped suddenly in 1974, but was revived in 1976 with the World Bank loan.[11] By 1980 survival rates in industrial plantation trials on 1,200 hectares were reported to be very uneven and were significantly lower than 76 percent—in some areas the new trees experienced 50 percent mortality, and many other trees showed immature growth. Again *P. caribaea (hondurensis)* performed better that the others tested. The 1968 pine experiments followed upon the judgment of the FAO and the Government of India that earlier experiments since 1962 to produce long-fiber requirements for paper mills from fast-growing eucalyptus plantations on 6,600 hectares had "not been successful except in some patches."[12] The eucalyptus data were so poor that forester O. P. Saxena, a manager of the Bastar project, suggested in 1976 that it "may not be feasible to wait until the end of the rotation of research and provenance trials."[13]

Unfortunately the results of their *P. caribaea* experiments in Bastar were not compared in the multisite analysis published in 1983 by the Commonwealth Forestry Institute at Oxford. At sixteen locations around the world, including the Jari project in Brazil, the productivity, flowering, and interaction with the environment of the Caribbean pines were evaluated: the variety *hondurensis* again proved superior to the others tested, and planners were advised to establish plantations of a minimum size of 500 hectares in order to grow and identify the best individuals from which to select breeding populations.[14] No site in India was mentioned, although Oxford experts had worked in the Bastar project. The need for such large clear-cut areas had already been established: Greaves reported *P. caribaea* to be incapable of regenerating itself in the shade of hardwood trees because all pines demand light.[15]

Not until 1984 was Plumptre's comprehensive report on Caribbean pine available; its evidence would suggest very mixed conclusions about this tree's quality. The plantation potential, though immediately recognized, was based on clear preconditions: "When plantations are established on good soils with initial cultivation and fire control, growth is very rapid indeed compared with growth in indigenous stands."[16] With often poor soils and no fire controls, Bastar did not meet these preconditions. "Considerable scope for breeding" was noted, but clearly this breeding had not occurred during the Bastar project. The worldwide evidence assembled by Plumptre showed high variation between individual trees, high variation in strength of trees under twenty years of age, and high variation between species. Although no veneers or plywoods had been produced commercially from Caribbean pine, pulp tests had shown it to be acceptable for mechanical, dissolving-grade pulps, or for semichemical and bisulphite pulps—although sap-staining, low brightness, and lower strengths were noted. Wood properties and pulp properties varied with the process. It was judged "marginal for the sack kraft range of papers." As a fuel, it burned quickly with lots of resinous sparks; as charcoal it produced high ash content. Juvenile trees in plantations, cut before twenty years, would not develop heartwood. Therefore, they would have unreliable structural strength for sawn logs. But the pine was deemed good for such products as rough furniture, flooring, packaging, and match boxes. Naturally grown trees were stronger, but were inferior to plantation trees in pulping performance. Plumptre concluded that the value of the pine in plantations could be lost unless wood and tree quality were taken into account. The doubts raised about Caribbean pine's performance in Bastar suggest it was not yet possible to meet certain optimistic quality conditions: "The prospects of obtaining any particular quality of wood are, therefore, quite good given the right sites and provenances, and the right silviculture and breeding techniques. The gains in quality as well as quantity are potentially large."[17]

The other source of long-fiber pulp material for paper in Bastar was bamboo, but by 1981 the FAO mission had concluded from all the preceding studies that its regeneration and supply were too uncertain due to the habit of bamboo to flower gregariously. Under these conditions, bamboo could not be clear-cut and left to regenerate. Bamboo plantations appeared necessary. Earlier experts had already pointed to the fact that data on bamboo in Bastar were inadequate for an investment decision. Throughout the project period, there was a small cut of bamboo in Bastar—30,000 tons annual average from 1977 through 1980, according to the Forest Department. This would have to expand enormously, with replanting begun on an equally large scale, to feed a pulp mill.

Forest Classification Issues. The area under control of the Forest Department during the project was 2.170 million hectares or 21,700 square kilometers: 985,000 hectares were classified as reserved forests, in which the department or corporation had exclusive rights; 1,185,000 hectares were classified as protected forest, in which tribals held nistari rights over 530,000 hectares (see table 6). Well over half the district was under the jurisdiction of the Forest Department. The basic question was which areas could be clear-cut and replanted with pine. Much of the protected forest had already been degraded, so focus was also upon the reserved forest. If the corporation gained access to it, the Forest Department's revenue would decline accordingly. In addition, "government policy" (set by the Forest Department) forbade the use of naturally regenerating zones of the forest for use of the (lower-valued) pine plantations. Only zones that did not regenerate naturally could be designated for clear-cutting and plantation development. "If the area currently classified as regenerating was to be substantially increased," said the 1981 FAO mission report, "this could seriously jeopardize the project."[18]

Obviously officials and experts were not in agreement, because until the end of 1980 final determination of the status of large areas of forest had not occurred. There was room for honest disagreement. Because longitudinal data on the Bastar forests were so scarce, and because

TABLE 6
Comparison of Forestry in Madhya Pradesh and Bastar
1976-1980

	Madhya Pradesh State	Bastar District
1. Total geographic area	442,841 km²	39,171 km²
2. Area under Forest Department control	166,161 km²	21,700 km²
3. Percent of total area under Forest Department	37.5%	55.3%
4. Percent of total area under forest	37.5%	57.0%
5. Forest classification		
Reserved Forest	48.2%	46.0%
Protected Forest	51.4%	54.0%
6. Dominant species		
Teak	18.8%	8.0%
Sal	22.8%	37.0%
Mixed	47.3%	37.0%
Bamboo	11.0%	18.0%

Source: Tomar and Saxena, *Souvenir of the Madhya Pradesh Forest Department*, 1976; and FAO/World Bank, *Draft Report of the India, Madhya Pradesh Commercial Forestry Development Project Preparation Mission*, April 1981:

much illegal (and thus unrecorded) forestry activity had occurred, it was very difficult to show which zones were not regenerating naturally. In spite of willingness on both sides to contemplate the problems, the issue of forest land classification was apparently so fundamental and so tied up with the uneasy relationship between the Forest Department and the corporation (staffed by officials seconded from the department) that its resolution became extremely difficult. This difficulty was compounded by the interpenetration of reserved forests and protected forests (after all, there was no fence), and by the demands of tribals and others for access. In fact, the ambiguity of the tribal status in the classification scheme constituted a third "technical" issue in the list of unresolved problems faced by development planners.

Tribal Status Issues. The nistari rights of tribals covered half a million hectares, effectively a quarter of the forest over which the Forest Department had jurisdiction in Bastar. The tribals could cut timber and poles for their own use, including firewood, and could collect minor forest products for sale exclusively to the department, now that such products were nationalized. In 1910 a special artificial "forest village" had been created in these forests, numbering 152 villages by 1980, from which the department obtained a supply of inexpensive, conveniently located labor.

Such labor service was obligatory in a forest village, which is a kind of labor camp. Although it was wage labour (the department paid Rs 5-10 per day), such labor could not be withheld: tenure in such villages was also at the pleasure of the Forest Department. These forest villages were not included in the jurisdiction of the Tribal Welfare Department. Each household was assigned ten acres for cultivation or forest products, but some acquired more. A nominal rent was charged, and where cultivation was good, people paid to get into forest villages. Where conditions were poor, the inhabitants were poor.

Tribals did not own the land on which their houses stood, and in addition some original tribal villages (distinct from forest villages) were destroyed at the time the forest villages were created. This arrangement led easily to exploitation of tribal labor by the department's officials and contractors alike, but it was not liked by all foresters. One official called it "antiquated," and said it "smacks of colonialism."[19] This view evidently percolated upward. By 1978 a conference of the central and state governments (including Madhya Pradesh) recommended the abolition of "forest villages," urging their conversion into ordinary "revenue villages" subject to the rest of the state's administrative apparatus—not under the exclusive jurisdiction of the Forest Department. This process of conversion was still under way at the end of the Bastar project. By the end of 1982, some 92 out of the district's 156 forest villages were to be converted: the remainder, in very remote areas, would be temporarily left under the Forest Department.

At the 1978 conference of Ministers of Tribal Welfare and Forestry, Prime Minister Indira Gandhi stressed the need to restore ecological balance in India by giving to the tribals a right over trees and a right to their use in specific assigned areas. The concept of nistari embraces the rights she desired, yet in Bastar as elsewhere these rights have been curtailed or otherwise limited. In a reserved forest, such rights extend only to satisfaction of personal/household needs and preclude the felling of timber, but in a protected forest, these strictures are relaxed. Without fences and other boundaries, tribals have de facto expectations of using the forest for their needs.

The demand for firewood illustrates this: the firewood problem became politically significant in India during the project period. Eventually, tribals would compete with others for their own needs if nistari rights were removed. In 1978, the World Bank estimated, India burned the equivalent of six million tons of nitrogenous fertilizer in the form of dung. Unable to substitute firewood for this valuable agricultural resource, India was burning more dung as fuel than was used by the current annual consumption of fertilizer. Although this problem was described as early as 1893 by Voelcker, it was now reaching crisis proportions. By late 1978 the Forest Department of Madhya Pradesh was forced to begin selling subsidized firewood in town shops in order to combat rising prices, hoarding, speculation, and illegal deforestation. The government's entry into the firewood business naturally generated concern within forestry circles; Eckholm quoted a Madhya Pradesh forest officer of the Bhopal district as saying, "We're drawing on our forest capital in order to meet today's needs. This can't go on forever."[20]

These government actions were based on a study done in 1977, showing that 26 of the 45 districts were already in a deficit of firewood. If trends continued 39 districts would be in a deficit by the end of the century.[21] Fuelwood plantations, with a planned employment potential of 60,000 people, were being designed by the department. The political pressure was great enough to cause the central government to strike a firewood study committee under the chairmanship of M. S. Swaminathan. The committee carried out its work during the period in which the TAP in Bastar was being evaluated.[22] Nevertheless, in 1981 a retired Inspector General of Forests said that 91 percent of wood production was being consumed as fuel in India. Partly for this reason, the World Bank had said in 1980 that it would lend $1 billion for fuelwood plantations around the world in 1981–1985: yet by 1981, Noronha of the World Bank was asking why it should be so difficult to grow fuelwood.[23]

The FAO mission estimated the cash value of minor forest products (Mfps) in Makdi to be between Rs 250 and Rs 500 per household. Yet at the national level the nistari right had few defendants. The National Commission on Agriculture had proposed to exclude increasing numbers of people from considerations of nistari, with the ultimate goal of abolishing nistari so as to deal effectively with clandestine removal and encroachment in forests.[24] In the interim, said the commission, nistari forests and other state forests should be separated as much as possible.

In addition to the cheap labor possibilities of the forest villages, there is the profitability of the forest products themselves. The FAO mission report notes that in 1979–1980 the Forest Department paid Rs 5.9 million to tribals for tendu patta leaves (for cigarettes). It then turned around and sold these same leaves to the market outside the district for Rs 12.6 million—over a 100 percent markup. In the case of harrar and sal seeds, a markup of 50–70 percent was found.[25] This high markup pattern is extended to every one of the resources removed from the forest. This economic activity, worth up to Rs 500 for some households in Bastar, goes along with nistari. If nistari is abolished, some or all of such income will decline.

On this matter of classification, the World Bank had declared itself at the same time as the National Commission on Agriculture, saying that "declaring areas as nistari forests alone is not sufficient to ensure that local people will not encroach on Reserved Forests."[26] It thus followed, said the Bank's project document, that "the rate at which categorization can proceed would be inhibited by the objections raised by local people." Therefore, much depends upon the concept of either social forests or nistari forests, and on the rights which forest dwellers have in them—a matter we will discuss in our recommendations. In spite of attempts to achieve a consensus, such as the Prime Minister's 1978 conference for Forestry and Tribal Welfare Ministers, there has been continued friction between the representatives and objectives of the Forest and Tribal Welfare Departments. In fact, how these predominantly tribal districts should be governed and administered has long been a serious question in the Indian Administrative Service.[27] It is plausible, therefore, that internal disagreement over these and other matters were translated into conflict over forestry projects in Bastar.

Forestry Development Corporation Issues. Could the new and inexperienced corporation successfully clear-cut, replant, and maintain thousands of hectares every year? Could it operate big industrial installations on a profitable basis? These were the kinds of questions being asked before the World Bank was to commit itself to a major investment in Bastar forestry. Because estimates of the size of the planned pulp mill varied, and because an additional sawmill had been proposed by Sandwell and the FAO mission, estimates of the extent of the annual cut varied: for the 100,000 ton mill, the annual planned cut was 2,000 hectares. Could a corporation that had cut 1,200 hectares in three or four project years, replanting some with pine, successfully manage the cutting and profitable replanting of 2,000 hectares every year, particularly given the uncertainties of weather and labor? The actual operation of a pulp mill and sawmill was new to this corporation, and there were no other public-sector enterprises in Madhya Pradesh with such experience. How big should it be? How many daily shifts could be successfully operated? The organization of the mill would influence its through put and thus the size of the annual cut. By 1980–1981 the withdrawal of private participation had left the MPFDC alone in the field.

Every year the area under intensive care would increase by at least 2,000 hectares. Firebreaks and fire roads would be needed at least every 200 hectares, and roads could be built only in the dry season—which was also the fire season. The tribals had been reported as warning of special fire hazards in the pine plantation, and this was subsequently confirmed by the FAO mission. Unfortunately the records of forest fires were not well kept, according to the National Commission on Agriculture: between 1960 and 1965, 1,260 forest fires in Madhya Pradesh had destroyed 58,899 hectares of forest.[28] The value of timber burned was recorded for only one year in this period, and for other years studied by the commission data were unavailable. The Commonwealth Forestry Institute had already concluded that because Caribbean pines thrive in freely drained soils, growing sites could dry out sufficiently during the dry season for ground fires to burn: therefore, only rarely could a pine plantation escape burning more than three successive years without fire-protection.[29] It was doubtful whether the logistical capabilities of the corporation would ever include maintaining the necessary water trucks and fire-warning and fire-fighting systems.

Finally, there was the issue of the MPFDC's profitability. While it had certainly not yet commenced full commercial operations, it was vulnerable to pressures from its parent, the Forest Department. In its first year (1976–1977) it made a profit of Rs 3.2 million on gross earnings of Rs 33.3 million. The following year it made a profit of only Rs 200,000 on gross earnings of Rs 49.7 million, partly because it had paid Rs 16 million in "lease rent" to the Forest Department.[30] The corporation's gross profit, after all, was being made from the same source to which the Forest Department needed access for revenue. The corporation was cutting and selling the department's assets, yet it was expecting (some would say presuming) that it would receive a glamorous new foreign investment. It must be remembered that the corporation's officers, its leadership, were simply on assignment from the department. Working for the corporation, in Bastar, was defined as a remote (hardship) posting for the Indian Forest Service. The foresters were paid a 20 percent salary premium, which foresters in other areas did not obtain. Doubts about the corporation or the department were also doubts about individual professionals and their capabilities. This divided situation, involving philosophies or attitudes toward the dramatic reorganization of the whole department, influenced the relative confidence placed in the capabilities of the new corporation.

This internal situation, reflected in the number of unresolved issues, was not confined to opinions about the Bastar project. The whole future of the use of forests in India was being debated, according to both the traditional philosophies of protection and conservation, code words in the tension between silviculture and the philosophy of industry. This tension was itself heightened by pressure upon diminishing resources. Some stated views among senior Indian officers were quite stark—for example, at an international conference in India in 1981:

This is the predicament. What can a handful of forestry personnel do to oppose the action of thousands of people who constantly nibble at the forest resources? The most important technical lag is that of organizational techniques on which rests the protection and productive functions of the forests. We are expecting too much from too few who, though competent, are overburdened with their tasks. At the same time, much depends on the good faith and goodwill of the people, and such goodwill can easily be dissipated if the parties had different perceptions of the nature of land development.

People have genuine demands and their expectation from the use of a resource cannot be tossed away. [31]

No less a figure than the Inspector General of Forests for the whole of India expressed at the same conference the mood within the forestry community. He addressed the impasse surrounding the clear-cutting of forests to be replaced by plantations. The forester's management practices, he said, "may be totally frustrated, creating conditions of abnormal stress and tension." This led him to question the current training and consequent attitudes of present-day forestry planners. The forest plantation, he said, illustrated precisely the inherent conflict:

> Let us consider another example of a natural forest predominantly of sal. This forest represents to poor forest-fringe-dwellers a source of livelihood yielding seeds for sale, branches and leaves for fuel and manure. The decision to convert this sal forest to industrially more valuable species like teak may satisfy the needs for higher revenues which may or may not be used for the welfare of these same people, but would certainly deprive them of an output from the forest which they were enjoying. [32]

He could not have spoken more directly to the issues in the continuation of the Bastar project.

Also during 1981 the world's most daring plantation forestry project, Jari in Amazonia, was declared a failure by its mysterious promoter Daniel Ludwig. Jari was sold to a group of private and government interests in Brazil. Foresters in India heard the Jari story at the 1981 conference, thus raising their suspicions regarding the transfer of exotic pine species to vast plantation projects. Already 100,000 hectares of a multispecies forest had been cut and replaced with Caribbean pine and gmelina, both fast-growing species.[33] Pine yields were half of those achieved in similar projects in other countries. Gmelina yields were 40 percent below target on the best soils, and were so poor elsewhere that the tree was being eliminated on lesser soils. Gmelina is a tree native to India, and plantations had been tried there in the 1930s. Only one crop rotation had been completed at Jari, but studies showed that all the potassium in the soil would be depleted following the second harvest. Yields were poor, and cultivation costs were higher than for other species. What is more, the monoculture had induced and accelerated insect and fungal outbreaks in the plantations. Economic and sociological problems associated with the project's enormous scale combined with these technical constraints to make the project inviable in Ludwig's eyes when the world price of pulp and paper fell in 1980–1981. His extreme secrecy promoted ill-feeling among Brazilians, and there were prolonged legal disputes over Ludwig's title to the property.

Among the influences upon the corporation and its parent Forest Department at the end of the Bastar project was the proposed Indian Forest Bill (1980). Prepared in 1978 by the Central Forestry Board, which coordinates the central and state governments, the draft of this bill was widely circulated through formal and informal channels but was not introduced in Parliament. In fact, wrote Kulkarni in 1983, "protagonists for the Bill are maintaining a solemn silence."[34] Even the Inspector General of Forests was reported as denying that the bill was anywhere near its final form.[35] Much public criticism of the draft focused on the draconian powers conferred on the Forest Department, but great power had long ago been transferred to department officials, according to tribals in the forests.

The proposed bill's fifteen chapters and 143 sections included provisions that could affect the corporation's plantation in an unpredictable and interactive way. After all, in the Bastar situation, greater *legislated* power was not what the corporation or department needed. From the tribal point of view, the new bill proposed more restriction on use of the forest—it would be an offense to remove grass, flowers, leaves, branches, fruit, and tubers, or to draw water or catch fish. Punishment on conviction would be up to three years' imprisonment and/or Rs 5,000; this could be doubled if the offense occurred between dusk and dawn. In spite of the fact that this bill was not introduced, it is clear that the cabinet of the Government of India was taking a direct interest in forests and specific forestry projects. In the words of the Minister of Agriculture in 1981, addressing an FAO conference, "No deforestation of Reserved Forests, or use of forest land for non-forestry purposes will be done without the prior approval of the Central Government."[36]

Taken together these issues help identify forces outside Bastar which contributed to the termination of the project, apart from the effect of the risk of tribal resistance and retaliation. Questions of forest classification, the nistari right, and the capabilities of the forest development corporation were affected by Bastar tribals only in a very shadowy way. These issues were created more by the interplay of national and local forces, and most particularly by international and national forces. Important as these problems were, we have concluded that some of them would have been overcome not only to continue but to expand the forestry project, had the majority of tribals been in favor of it. What is more, had tribals been involved in the project from the start, they themselves might have helped to resolve such issues as the survival of seedlings in plantations, productivity of seed nurseries, preparations for fire fighting, and the supply of labor. With their knowledge of forests and trees, and with their labor, these difficulties might have been overcome. But as we have shown, the tribals were ignored by the forestry project. The tribals were simultaneously preoccupied with a set of challenges to their own economic and political future. Since they believed the project would not become part of their future, their indifference turned to opposition. Thus, the corporation had to face a set of unpredictable market, legislative, and silvicultural obstacles entirely on its own.

CHAPTER 7

The Risk of Tribal Resistance and Retaliation

In January 1982, armed with their traditional bows and arrows, some 300 tribals forced forest officials to unload trucks carrying timber in the Mandapal forest [of Bastar]. When a police party went to arrest the people involved, it was surrounded by armed tribals which led to a police firing. Three days later, 50 armed tribals surrounded a police station and demanded the release of their arrested colleagues. —*The State of India's Environment*, 1982

IN THE World Bank's initial funding document, just above the place for Robert McNamara's signature, the Bank's executive directors were warned as follows: "A major risk that may affect the projects expected to follow from the feasibility study would be suspicion and lack of co-operation from the tribals in the project area."[1] Not only might tribals not present themselves for work in the project, but they also might hinder the work of others. Evidence suggests that some people anticipated even more direct opposition. The distinction between the oral and the documentary traditions in the project means that these risks were regularly acknowledged in conversation, though seldom in writing. Most participants knew something of the legendary capacity of Bastar people to resist unfavorable changes and, at times, to retaliate against those who seemed to be responsible for them. Only ten years before the project began, the district capital of Jagdalpur had been seized by a massive and violent confrontation between thousands of tribal bowmen and a large contingent of rifle-bearing government military forces. The reasons for this confrontation, to be detailed below, had to do with the chronic disregard and, in most quarters, the profound ignorance with which relations were conducted between the local administration and state government, on the one hand, and the tribal people of Bastar, on the other.

Both foreigners and Indian nationals involved in the Bank's project spoke of the tribals' suspicion and said something should be done to win their cooperation. Although they might not take this initiative themselves, it was widely felt "somebody" should. The few activities in this direction (beekeeping, etc., described above) can be understood as driven by this feeling. A few observers said it was too little too late; others genuinely believed that, once the industrial projects proceeded, their scale would be large enough to absorb the tribals or allow them to coexist, as they wished.

Nonetheless, one could imagine a pulp mill or sawmill deep in the forest, under siege, with access roads blocked and nontribal laborers afraid to work or travel. One plan was to locate the pulp mill in the heavily forested Barsur area. It took little imagination to foresee the tactics of tribal resistance used in other parts of India being imported to Bastar, despite seasoned assurances that "these Bastar tribals are not really like the others." The fact that firearms were not yet in extensive use, but eventually might be, could not have escaped the attention of any planner who guessed the extent of tribal antipathy to the TAP as it was proceeding.

For the most part, this perception of tribal mistrust was explained in terms of "a nice but backward people," who could not grasp (i.e., were not capable of understanding) the distinct possibility of a positive outcome for them in the project. Limited by a lack of education and comparative experience, the explanation went, and committed to an outmoded way of life, tribals mistrusted what they did not understand. That is why they were not cooperative. It was for other nontribal people to refer with contempt to tribals as *kam chor* (lazy) or *sharabi* (drunkards). Such people needed to announce their superiority by reminding the tribals of their place. Though this perhaps occurred at the lower levels of the TAP, at the expert level, we believe, there was a wide range of perceptions, from those who understood the logic of tribal mistrust to those who believed the project would roll successfully over any suspicion. Such a range was reflected in the plans and studies done just before the project commenced; the indifference of the Tewari and Susaeta industrial plans contrasts strikingly with the more sensitive reports to the Ford Foundation by Reynolds and Aurora.

A highly public event during the TAP served to remind planners of the risks in setting industrial projects deep within Bastar. In early 1978 the police shot and killed many strikers at the Bailadila iron ore mine. Some of those killed were nontribals, but tribal housing near the mine was set on fire by police. A high-level inquiry brought Bastar's social relations onto the main stage of the national media. A mass-circulation report described four days of provocation and confrontation between mine workers and the Central Industrial Security Force, including the use of clubs and tear gas.[2] During the course of arrests, workers beat up some policemen, one of whom died. The security force retaliated immediately, shooting dozens of people, setting fire to workers' camps, and raping women. At least eleven people died, and sixty-five were hospitalized with injuries. It was widely believed that other bodies had been quickly removed and buried. The Minister of Tribal Welfare rushed to Bastar, as did numerous other political leaders—but it was all over. The caution voiced in 1973, projecting the iron ore mine experience, had been fully realized.

In a study of Dantewada tehsil surrounding the mine, in the same year as the shooting, evidence showed not only that crime was increasing in the tehsil but that tribals were committing crimes more frequently than nontribals, particularly property-related crimes like theft and burglary. This report suggested that tribals were often falsely implicated in crimes committed by others, or that they were induced to commit them by others.[3] They may also have been caught more easily, or the records may have focused on them more than on others. These crimes were, of course, separate from the regular tribal violations of forest regulations. Whatever the case, a project mixing tribal and nontribal workers, where there would be the usual violence associated with industrial disputes, would probably develop patterns like the ones at Bailadila—unless, of course, very special efforts were made from the beginning to avoid them. This was not the case, however.

One year after the 1978 Bailadila massacre, as it became known, a story critical of the project was published in a design and planning magazine with an elite distribution in India.[4] It did not speak of the possibility of tribal violence, but listed all the other arguments against the project which were being publicly discussed. Written by a Sharad Varma, a local journalist unpopular among project officials, the article disturbed the usually quiet forestry community and sent ripples all the way to New Delhi and Washington, D.C. One conclusion reached by Varma was as follows:

The Project will smash this social structure and increase social inequalities. The surprising thing is that although they are aware of the serious implications of the Pine Project, the authorities prefer to shut their eyes. Have pine forests become so essential that the lives and well-being of 1,400,000 tribals can be sold up the river? What compulsions and what false prestige are behind this excess? [5]

In addition, a distinguished anthropologist, respected by the central and state governments in India and noted for his optimism regarding the future of tribal people in Bastar (see chapter five), concluded that the project was "an extreme example of [the] commercialization of forests at the expense of the local tribal population."[6] Both the 1980 tribal study and the report by the FAO avoided mention of the possibility of tribal retaliation, but suspicion and noncooperation (anticipated by Robert McNamara) were central themes. This must surely have been the process through which the continuation of the project became politically contentious.[7] But one must remember that the project evolved in a wider context, not only of tribal relations in Bastar and Madhya Pradesh, but in many other Indian states as well. Conflict, sometimes violent, between the central government, state government, and tribal populations was public knowledge during the years in which this project was being evaluated.

In Bastar alone, following the spectacular events of 1966 investigated by the Pandey Commission, the politics of the tribal relation to non-tribal people had grown complicated and was periodically tense. A short review of Bastar political history will be helpful in clarifying these relations. As mentioned in our introduction, before Indian independence and the merger of the princely states, Bastar polity was in the form of a monarchy headed by a king considered divine by his mostly tribal subjects. The relationship between the king and the tribals was a very important one, since the king was ultimately and devoutly held responsible for the prosperity and well-being of his people—as well as for the resources on which they depended. To illustrate this relationship, we may refer to the events of 1876—the occasion of the visit of the Prince of Wales to India.

As a recognized feudatory of the British Empire, the then monarch of Bastar, Raja Bhairam Deo, was expected to meet the Prince of Wales in Bombay. Before he was to leave, the force of the institution of divine kingship intervened in Bhairam Deo's plans. The intervention came in the form of about 10,000 Gonds (Murias and Bhattras), who laid seige to the palace for several weeks and refused to allow their divine benefactor to leave the kingdom. Fearing disruption in the cycle of prosperity and stability guaranteed by the king's presence, the Gonds vigorously protested against his departure and also against their being left in the hands of some of his ministers, who had acquired a notorious reputation for tribal oppression. The attendants of one of these ministers overreacted to the protests, shooting and killing some of the Muria tribals. Eventually a large detachment of the Indian Army arrived to quell the presumed insurrection. The Political Agent for Bastar arrived soon after. Upon relating to him their grievances, the tribals received satisfaction to the extent that the accused ministers were banished and order was restored within a few days.[8]

But British influence on Bastar and British interest in the development of Bastar's forest wealth did not abate. Continuing trouble within the kingdom and the declining effectiveness of Bhairam Deo's rule led to the virtual supersession of the old king by 1886. Upon his death in 1891, the British assumed full administration of Bastar.[9] Grigson, with his close perspective on the administrative history of the state, describes this period as one of escalating turmoil, economic oppression, and disruption of traditional practices:

From 1886 to 1891 and for the first few years of the long (1891–1908) minority of Raja Rudra Pratap Deo, a series of subordinate officials were lent as Diwans (chief ministers) to the State, and a further evil arose in the growing array of minor State officials abusing the ancient custom of *bisaha*, or the payment by villagers of a twentieth of their crops for the feeding of the Raja's servants, by interpreting it as a right to commandeer any aboriginal's produce at an arbitrarily fixed and often nominal price, and generally forgetting to pay even that. The newly-cleared roads seemed to run through wilderness, for on villagers of roadside villages the burden of *begar*, or forced labour, and bisaha fell with especial severity. Being 184 miles from Raipur, the headquarters of the Commissioner and the Political Agent, Bastar was seldom visited, and the people were far too much at the mercy of the incompetence or knavery of the local officials. The latter meanwhile were carrying out the prescribed policy of opening communications, introducing the criminal police and judicial system of British India, and exploiting the forests (again by forced labour).[10]

Along with the new officialdom, the lower ranks of which "regarded service in a native state only as a means to the rapid acquisition of wealth,"[11] there came the new immigrants. As stated earlier, these were Hindu and Muslim agriculturalists who were encouraged to settle in Bastar and to expand permanent cultivation. Easily taking advantage of their opportunities, the first wave of these immigrants soon found themselves as nominal landlords or lessees over long-established tribal villages, and over the heads of traditional headmen. So established

> the lessees at once proceeded as fast as possible to get the best land into their own hands . . . to ignore the use and wont of village life, especially the *sari-bori* or co-operation in supplies and labour for village bread-winning and village festivals, to introduce Hindu and Mussalman settlers, and to turn the natives of Bastar into bondservants little better than slaves by advancing them money, on terms which made repayment practically impossible, in return for labour or that of their sons.[12]

Although there was a short period of amelioration of these conditions near the turn of the century, by the end of the first decade many of these same abuses of "modernization" regained currency. The renewed tribal discontent eventually resulted in the 1910 rebellion, which, as recounted above, broke out with a vehemence that underscored tribal hostility to immigrant exploiters and the demand to keep Bastar for Bastar forest-dwellers.[13]

The ensuing long period of close and careful British management kept Bastar quiet and more or less stable until some years after Indian independence. The conditions which undermined this stability and which culminated in the upheaval of 1966 also were rooted in divine kingship, or more precisely, in the importance of divine kingship to the Gonds of Bastar. The last king of Bastar, a charismatic and highly influential figure among the tribals, was able legitimately to sit on his throne for only a matter of months before being deposed by the newly independent Government of India in 1948. At first apparently reconciled to his deposition, Maharajah Pravir Chandra Bhanj Deo soon made it clear that he considered the new regime a poor substitute for his own management of Bastar and its people. (In the 1930s the Kakatiya kings of Bastar had been elevated to the rank of Maharajah.) His activities and pronouncements in the early 1950s were full of vitupera-tive denunciation of the new government, of the Congress party, and of what he considered to be the corrupt officialdom of the Bastar adminis-tration. This he contrasted with the benevolent politesse of former

British suzerainty and the natural superiority of divine monarchy in a traditional state. His autobiography, *I Pravir: The Adivasi God* (1965), sets out these opinions in an unrestrained manner.

Needless to say, the government took a rather dim view of Pravir's inclinations and soon began its own campaign to discredit him. Accusing him of depravity and irresponsibility as well as many of the other negative stereotypes of Indian royalty, the government capped its case by declaring him a megalomaniac.[14] These "findings" were deemed sufficient to justify declaring Pravir incompetent because of mental infirmity and to place his estate under the Court of Wards in 1953. Shocked into silence at first, Pravir later responded that "the people of Bastar took resentment against the Government order."[15] He thus revealed his assumption that he was not without a following. His next step, which was to enter the political arena proper, showed that this assumption was well-founded.

By 1957 Pravir and a select group of mainly tribal followers were elected to the Legislative Assembly of Madhya Pradesh. But Pravir's immediate goal—to have his estate returned to him—was not thus achieved. Resigning in protest, Pravir then formed a new all-tribal party, which took to a course of protest and demonstration. In 1960 the Chief Minister of Madhya Pradesh asked Pravir to leave the district and take up residence elsewhere. Pravir's answer was threatening: "If Government are not careful, there may be a rebellion here. . . . Kindly note that I am not joking; the matter may become serious."[16] When the press noted the possibility of his "de-recognition," Pravir's warnings became even more dire.[17]

At the level of government perception, most of Pravir's statements were taken as little more than disgruntled bombast. Nehru is quoted as having said that the Bastar situation was "hardly a situation, but a matter for a District Magistrate to deal with."[18] Heedless of this downplaying by the Prime Minister, Pravir traveled to Delhi to present his grievances in person. These grievances, which criticized the local Congress party leaders and administration of Bastar and accused them of misappropriating development funds while they neglected tribal interests, were sternly disregarded by the Home Minister. Some weeks later, as he was reentering his former kingdom, Pravir was arrested, taken to a jail outside the district, and in rapid follow-up on 11 February 1961, was derecognized as the Maharajah of Bastar.

If the government considered these actions sufficient to subvert the escalation of the Bastar problem, it was probably guided by the Prime Minister's assumption that the Bastar kingship was a personal rather than a social matter. This assumption had already been belied by Pravir's successful foray into electoral politics, which had been effected through substantial tribal support. That such support was based on traditional charismatic (in the sociological sense of the word) relationships was an insight to which the government blinded itself by insisting on viewing those relationships in modernistic terms.

In March 1961 the news of Pravir's removal brought together a large number of tribals (reported at 10,000) at a village near Jagdalpur to demand his immediate release. Mostly from areas closely surrounding the capital, these tribals, predominantly Bhattra, Raja Muria, and Bisonhorn Maria, voiced their protests in traditional and indigenous forms. They declared that unless Pravir were released and allowed to return to Bastar,"their crops would fail, their cattle would die and other calamities would fall on them."[19] The officials, who had come out to the village Lohandiguda in order to confront and disperse the gathering, attributed no importance to what they called adivasi superstitions. Unable to placate the tribals (let alone penetrate the language barrier), the officials proclaimed their assembly unlawful and ordered the police to fire tear gas. The situation got out of control and "became riotous," according to police officials. Subsequent gunfire resulted in the killing of twelve tribals. A number of tribals were later rounded up and committed to stand trial for attempted murder. Acquitting all the accused, the magistrate concluded that much of the evidence was "entirely artificial, [and] bristling with improbabilities."[20] Within a few weeks of the 1966 Lohandiguda firing, as it became known in Bastar, Pravir was released from jail on the grounds of insufficient cause for his detention.

Focusing his attention on the general elections of 1962, Pravir then formed the Akhil Bharatiya Maharaja party. He drew upon his tribal support for membership and began a campaign for his chosen candidates. Although he himself lost the election, most of his candidates were returned, and the attention thus generated swelled the ranks of his followers. By 1963 more and more tribals began to come to Jagdalpur to congregate at Pravir's palace. Nervously perceiving imminent trouble, the authorities tried to restrict these gatherings of tribals armed with bows and arrows, which again touched off violent confrontation. This time, however, the target was reached. Two months after a tribal occupation of the Court of Wards, the state government directed the Court of Wards to relinquish the superintendence of Pravir's estate. Pravir celebrated this success by lavishly displaying his royal prerogative, which was to distribute large sums of money to his followers.

Continuing to spend freely throughout the rest of 1963, Pravir also gave a number of press interviews that demonstrated his overarching ambition to reinstate kingship. On 12 October he stated that the tribals had in mind to declare Bastar a separate state, independent of the Indian Union and the Indian government, with himself as the ruler. This was, of course, courting disaster—but by this time Pravir was unable to halt the momentum of his own successful charisma. The demand for the reconstitution of Bastar as an independent Hindu-tribal monarchy continued throughout 1964, 1965, and part of 1966.

Throughout the same time period, the solidarity between Pravir and his tribal followers continued to grow. The strength of this solidarity in turn implied a growing sense of separation from the Indian state. This was organized by Pravir into an innovative set of roles modeled on political party idioms. He selected leading tribal men and women from numerous villages in Jagdalpur, conferred upon them the titles of *member* and *memberin*, and supplied them with insignia—these being the traditional media of affiliation—such as red cloth (saris) for the women memberins. To those selected who were already area headmen (*pargana manjhi*), he gave the title Raja Manjhi and distributed blue turbans. Their assistants (*chalki*) were given yellow livery and the designation Raja Chalki. Even the village watchmen (*kotwar*) were incorporated, receiving the raja title and invested with rose-hued turbans. It should be noted that the most politically involved followers of Pravir were those with least access to forest areas; that is, the rice-cultivating Muria, Raja Muria, Bhattra, and Bison-horn Maria of Jagdalpur, Kondagaon, and Dantewada tehsils.

On reviewing these actions, a government-appointed investigator, Justice K.L. Pandey, commented adversely: "All these Adivasis, particularly the memberins, worked with a great zeal if only to prove that they were worthy of the distinctions conferred on them. They were always ready and willing to carry out any direction given by Pravir Chandra Bhanj Deo. Although he had done precious little for the

Adivasis, he did not hesitate to wantonly use them as tools for his own purposes."[21] Unfortunately, the superficiality of this statement is matched only by its poverty of comprehension. That Justice Pandey ultimately must be considered a government servant is of course relevant here, especially in that his perception of the Bastar social world could only with great difficulty grant validity to tribal reliance on divine kingship. Written not so long before the events described here, and thus available, in theory at least, for planners' consideration, the following statement even if taken into account would be unlikely to have been understood by any of them:

> The Maharaja is regarded as divine by all the Muria and Maria. . . . So strongly do the aboriginals believe this, that they greatly resent the Maharaja leaving the State even for a short time. His absence means a withdrawal of divine protection from cattle, crops and people.[22]

It would be wrong to take this as an indictment of modern Indian officialdom for not having an anthropological understanding. Nevertheless, acting on this knowledge, instead of dismissing it as exploited credulity, might have saved the administration much trouble.

At any rate, more trouble was on its way. In the drought-filled agricultural year of 1965–1966, the Madhya Pradesh government imposed a graded levy on rice production in all rice-growing districts of the state, including Bastar, whose administration complied with it unquestioningly. For Bastar this meant ignoring the fragilities of tribal paddy cultivation, which not only yielded a quantity much below average but was also not geared to surplus production. Whatever paddy the tribals could save was intended to be used in the very lean monsoon months, when in fact most tribals turned to wild forest produce as the final hedge against starvation.

In the event, it was concluded that the imposition of the levy "caused genuine hardship to the small cultivators of Bastar district . . . [for the additional reasons that the] quantities required to be levied on their outturn, unrelated as they were to actual outturn, were fixed ad hoc solely for the purposes of procurement without taking into account either the expenses incurred for raising the crop or the number of dependents on individual cultivators."[23] It could scarcely be surprising that the Bastar tribal cultivators' response to the levy was in the main noncompliant, in some cases violently so.

This refusal to cooperate in the levy was organized and focused by Pravir's tribal members and memberins. Pervasive as this issue was, it readily lent itself to large-scale opposition to the administration. Perhaps more than any other single contention, the rice levy increased the breadth and depth of Maharaja-tribal interactions. Greater than ever before, the numbers of tribal people coming and going to and from Jagdalpur, and carrying out various disruptive strategies, created a highly apprehensive atmosphere in the capital. Furthermore, extending far beyond Jagdalpur, though tactically emanating from there, these tribal activities of noncooperation prompted authorities to prepare militarily for a major conflagration.

By the end of February 1966, matters had become even more tense as the antigovernment agitations spread to include the obstruction of all government operations, from the preparation of voter lists to the nonpayment of taxes. In addition, in March, the celebration of the *Chaitrai* festival brought unprecedentedly large numbers of tribals to Jagdalpur to gather at the king's palace. That most arrived armed with bows and arrows, though not illegally so, increased the nervousness of the authorities and police. A rapidly approaching sense of climax began to overtake the situation, although on the surface a cool front was adopted, particularly by officials who took the opportunity to remove themselves from the vicinity of Jagdalpur.

On 25 March an order was promulgated "which prohibited, for a period of fourteen days, all processions and meetings, assembly of five or more persons and the possession or keeping of bows, arrows, lathis [bamboo staffs] and other lethal weapons within the limits of Jagdalpur Municipality and also within a radius of five miles." [24] This was ordered because the police had learned of speeches delivered to the amassed tribals by two Samyukta Socialist party politicians, urging them to take out a procession through the town further to remonstrate over their grievances. Armed police parties were posted at the palace entrances and a precautionary vigil was begun. In the palace at the time were a score of prisoners under trial, incarcerated at the judicial jail. One of these prisoners started a commotion that attracted the attention of a group of tribals camped in the adjacent grounds. The escort guards took rough action against the approaching group of tribal men, which provoked them to retaliate with a volley of arrows, overcoming the police defenders. The jail was then smashed open, the prisoners were released, and the prison guards were chased out of the palace grounds.

At the main gate, the tribals encountered the police party stationed there to enforce the above-mentioned order. This party was also fought, and tear gas and rifle fire forced the tribals to retreat. While retreating, the tribals returned the rifle fire with arrow shots, wounding one policeman and killing another. Enraged and apparently completely out of control, the police chased the tribal group through the palace gardens and into the palace buildings. It was at this point when Pravir, coming out onto his porch to see what was going on, was shot and killed, along with eleven tribals. Such, at least, was the finding produced by Justice Pandey at the conclusion of his commission of inquiry.[25]

The early aftermath of Pravir's death was one of shock, confusion, and severe demoralization—a state of affairs most pronounced among the tribal communities. Among the officials, there was fear of a dangerous backlash from the tribals once it became generally known that their god-king had been killed. Curiously (perhaps because of this fear), now that he was dead, the authorities granted more significance to Pravir's divinity than when he was alive. To prevent what was anticipated as potential large-scale tribal violence all over the district, the authorities devised the ruse of having a local man impersonate the Maharaja and had him driven around Jagdalpur and along the main roads of Bastar in the royal Rolls Royce. As another precaution, a palace *munshi* (clerk-messenger) was given the task of spreading the "news" that Pravir had not died in the gunfire but was proceeding to take refuge or exile in the jungle.

Within a year or two, rumors began to circulate that Pravir had returned and that he was to be found at Chapka, a village some fifteen miles from Jagdalpur. Up to this point, it was still not accepted that he had actually been killed—so when it was found that the man at Chapka did not bear much resemblance to Pravir, nor had his fair complexion, the explanation was given that his skin had become darkened from the smoke of gunfire during the palace shooting. To further substantiate the story, scars on the man's body were pointed out which were said to be from bullet wounds sustained in the firing.

As more and more tribals flocked to Chapka to see this transformed Pravir, the story began to change. It came at last to be believed that Pravir had in fact died, and that he had been martyred for the moral transgressions of tribal people. His return was as an *avatar*, a reincarnation of the divine in the form of a *sadhu*—a Hindu mendicant named Baba Bihari Dass.

To pay for and redeem their "sins," the tribals were told that they had to give up traditional practices considered immoral, such as drinking liquor, dancing, and eating meat. As a sign of this expiation, they were encouraged to wear a bead sacred to Vaisnava Hindus—called *Kanti* beads—which cost them Rs 1.25 each, a not insignificant sum to most tribal people. At the same time, many tribal women, attracted by the charismatic accessibility offered by "Kanti-wallah Baba," as Bihari Dass was known in the beginning, took to such Hindu symbols as *sindhor*, the streak of red powder worn along the central part in the hair to indicate married status.

The happenings at Chapka drew increasing attention from all corners of Bastar. By early 1969 district officials and local journalists began to view the developments at Chapka in a serious light. Considering Kanti-wallah Baba's alarming, widespread popularity—at the height of his influence, he had an estimated 400,000 followers—they decided they had better find out who this man really was.

In fact, no one really knew. It was never admitted to most outsiders that he was considered an avatar of Pravir. Nor did the man himself reveal anything of his identity except his name, Baba Bihari Dass, and, vaguely, his origins as a *sadhu*, or holy man, from northern India. Even this information, upon attempted verification, proved either unreliable or false. When questioned as to what he was doing, he simply replied that he was trying to "uplift" the tribals, to work for their moral improvement. His questioners were not particularly satisfied with these responses, feeling that Bihari Dass was perpetrating a huge fraud, a successful confidence game by which he was winning a considerable fortune. Despite their suspicions, however, the officials could find nothing illegal in Bihari Dass's activities.

Taking a fresh tack, the Collector of Bastar, who was both a protribal idealist and an orthodox Brahmin, decided to co-opt Bihari Dass. In accordance with his own biases, he covertly tried to enlist Bihari Dass to emphasize further the proscriptions against liquor and meat—*mand-mas*, as they were idiomatically rendered in Halbi. Not wishing publicly to endorse Bihari Dass, or to appear to be giving him official sanction, the Collector approached him indirectly through his main tribal associates as well as through the old palace munshi, who were now important functionaries in Bihari Dass's growing organization. With little need of persuasion, the Baba readily accepted the Collector's tacit support.

He did more than accept it. With increased confidence gained from the unofficial encouragement bestowed upon him by Bastar's most powerful political figure, the Baba strengthened the force of his exhortations by threatening excommunication for those who refused to wear the Kanti (adding that all fish caught by transgressors would turn to stone). In addition, he enlarged the symbolic efficacy of his already millennial myth by foretelling a long seventy-two-hour night of doom, during which would occur the final judgment and punishment for all sinners. Only those, it was said, who disposed of all the black objects in their possession, including their black livestock (such as chickens, sheep, goats, cattle, and water buffalo) would be saved from eternal damnation.

It is important to note that this was not an unprecedented event. It was, in fact, an almost exact repeat of an earlier occurrence:

> In 1932 a rumour went through all the tribes of Jeypore and spread thence to Bastar that a god had descended on one of the mountains of the Eastern Ghats and commanded all men to give up keeping black poultry and goats, wearing clothes or using umbrellas or blankets with any black in them, and using beads or articles made of aluminium alloy. The message was rapidly bruited abroad, and everywhere villages had *bohorani* (disease-riddance) ceremonies for purifying themselves from disease, and cast out black goats, cocks, hens, umbrellas, blankets, *waskats* (waistcoats), beads, aluminum ornaments and domestic utensils on the village boundary. Mohammedans began to make a good thing out of slaughtering the goats or exporting them. Strenuous propaganda by the State soon stopped this impoverishing rumour, and some of the villagers in the end recovered much of their property from the police, who had been ordered to take charge of it.[26]

In 1970 most of these same circumstances also netted lucrative profits for nontribal middlemen, but to a greater extent, as the Bastar administration was now initially hamstrung by its behind-the-scenes complicity. When the Collector finally did react to the Chapka millennium, the new moral order, he did so in a sharp and direct manner, seizing—without much in the way of counterpropaganda—all the livestock the tribals were losing in give-away transactions. Such transactions were compounded by the inequities of the malik makbooja system, through which the same nontribal middlemen bought trees from individual tribals for Rs 5 and resold them to timber merchants for Rs 300. All of this was done with the complicity of government officials in Bastar, particularly in the field offices out in the district.

For the Baba, the Collector's intervention was not a great setback. It had minimal effect on the ideological commitments of Bihari Dass's followers, since, as tribals, they were generally and often vehemently predisposed to see the administration as one of their worst enemies. In this context, the Baba was easily able to extend and deepen his influence to the point where he began acting as an alternate administration. It was simply a matter of exercising his royal prerogative, as the Maharaja's avatar, to act as the authority and arbiter in tribal affairs. Thus, he assumed the role of judge in any problems or disputes that were brought before him. Unencumbered by the delays and confusions of formal judicial process, the Baba's dispensations were increasingly sought. He continued to press for tribal reform and the mand-mas prohibition. In addition, he imposed fines in the settlement of village disputes; he also imposed (and collected) fines when he found the individuals concerned, or anyone else, not wearing his Kanti bead. Furthermore, along with his own spear-carrying, khaki-wearing police force, Bihari Dass made himself available for village tours, as the Maharaja had done. Each tour required a large monetary retainer.

Deeming these extensions of influence to be a thoroughly unacceptable usurpation of official powers, the Bastar administration instituted various court cases against Bihari Dass. His subsequent arrest led to massive reaction by the tribals. Large numbers came to Jagdalpur in his support, held protest demonstrations and agitations and generally created a very tense atmosphere entirely reminiscent of the days before the palace firing that had killed Pravir. At this point (early February 1972), the Collector ordered Bihari Dass to leave the district within seven days. But before the month was out, the Collector himself was removed from office, was given one day's notice, and was required to leave the district.

The reasons for this abrupt reversal were relatively simple: the fear of a recurrence of the incidents of 1966, and, in light of imminent elections, the outcome of covert vote-bargaining between Bihari Dass and the Madhya Pradesh (Congress party) Chief Minister. In a further recapitulation of Pravir's career, Bihari Dass won several seats for the Congress party in 1972. During the campaign it was reported that, for the declared quarter-rupee Congress party membership fee, the Baba demanded a full rupee from the money-poor tribals. This is mentioned not so much to emphasize tribal exploitation, but to indicate its journalistic origins. In general, the press exerted an all-out attack on Bihari Dass, selecting in characteristic fashion the smears of moral decrepitude and salacious depravity as the main weapons of assault. In 1973 newspapers carried the story that Bihari Dass had made pregnant two of his attendant tribal girls.

While many such allegations against him were widely accepted as true by nontribals, Bihari Dass's following remained strong and united. Moreover, having acquired legitimate status in the modern political sphere, he now proceeded even more vigorously to capture the spiritual title to Bastar. This included redirecting the district ceremonial and ritual center to Chapka, where he had a new chariot built for the celebration of the Dasara. Riding atop the chariot in the position of the king, Bihari Dass's enactment of the Dasara came closest to proclaiming himself explicitly as the royal incarnation. His duplication of the functions of the Bastar kings included the selling of the sacred thread. Later, declaring the stream flowing alongside his Chapka headquarters to be as "pure" as the River Ganges, he sold bottles of holy water to his visitors. Followers were convinced of the efficacy of the Baba's Hindu guarantees of spiritual/temporal power—the power to manifest the New Age under the mantle of the old order of divine kingship.

Beyond the millennial pale, however, political events were soon to overtake the progress of Bihari Dass in Bastar. His Congress party superiors realized that the Baba's overwhelming dominance over Bastar was a source of much coveted favor, yet it also was a threat to any control over him. They played a double game, extending one hand in supplication while holding in the other the cloaked dagger. The coup de grace came in 1975 during the "Emergency Period", when Bihari Dass was arrested and jailed for two years under the Maintenance of Internal Security Act. His property was seized, the activities at Chapka were brought to a standstill, and his close tribal following was dispersed. The Baba Bihari Dass movement subsided into a state of uncertainty and waiting. But this did not end the story of Baba Bihari Dass. His movement started again after his release from prison and continues up to the time of this writing, albeit in weakened form—the Baba now justifies his leadership as a kindling of modern socioeconomic awareness among the adivasis of Bastar.

In light of the foregoing, and in light of the greater context of the political and historical background of the Bastar forestry project, such projects can be seen to carry extreme risk of tribal resistance. In fact, shortly after the announcement of a proposed review of "the controversial World Bank–aided Pine Plantation projects,"[27] tribal resistance did indeed break out in 1981 and 1982, even as the decision to terminate the project was being considered. As reported in the *Indian Express*, 7 February 1982:

> The Madhya Pradesh Government is perturbed over reports of an armed revolt by tribals and the setting up of a parallel authority in parts of Bastar district. Armed with bows and arrows, the tribals have stood up against the forest and government officials in some remote villages of the district, not allowing them to fell trees and carry timber from nationalised forests.[28]

Similarly, in the *Hindu*, 14 February 1982:

> Echoes of a "rebellion" are heard in Bhopal from the distant, tribal-dominated Bastar. This time the slogan is not to allow timber from the forests of Bastar to be exported but to keep it for use by the tribals. . . . The tribals believe that the forests belong to them and that they have the divine right to appropriate forest produce for their existence. The privileges of cutting trees for fuel, implement-making and house-building . . . and of enjoying the forest produce have been theirs from the days of Raja Annam Deo. They want these rights to be restored now and protest against the enforcement of the "jungle laws" of the Forest Department. The protest led to a series of events culminating in police firing near Kondagaon . . . where a few days back, a crowd of about 300 tribals stopped 10 truckloads of timber in the Mardapal forest area. . . . It is alleged that Baba Beharidas, who has a history behind him, is fanning the flames of discontent among the adivasis.[29]

There can be little doubt, given this situation and its history, that a major, if not the prime, reason for the cancellation of the Bastar forestry project was the threat of tribal resistance and retaliation. Without a thoroughgoing program of long-term tribal preparation and involvement through realistic communication, it is unlikely that any similar project in the future could succeed. Only with such long-term preparation might the whole issue of their rights in the forest, as dealt with in our concluding chapter, be settled in a manner convincing to them.

It turns out that tribal people did take a hand in the decision to terminate. In 1981 tribal Members of Parliament, in and outside Bastar, presented Prime Minister Indira Gandhi with some of the evidence regarding the Bastar forestry project. She responded by creating a small task-force, which interviewed the Chief Minister and Minister of Forests of Madhya Pradesh, a former Collector of Bastar (an expert on tribal development), and the MPFDC's officials. Chaired by Inspector General of Forests M. K. Dahlvi, the task-force contained one tribal member of Parliament from Orissa as well as forestry and environmental experts. It not only interviewed important persons but also reviewed the final World Bank and FAO reports and the finances of the MPFDC. The approach of the chairman and others is reported to have been to use this occasion to make positive and constructive recommendations and have them implemented, thus testing or strengthening sections of the new forest bill circulating in draft form at the time. The task-force recommended cancellation of the pine plantation project and approval of a scaled-down version of the pulp and paper mill (about half the proposed size of 100,000 tons per annum). This mill would be fed by bamboo, the existing forest, and (perhaps) small pine plantations grown on the land already clear-cut by the corporation: 50 percent of the shares in this mill were recommended to be owned by the tribal development cooperatives of Bastar. What role the corporation was expected to play is unclear. The task-force reported directly to the Prime Minister who, according to reliable sources, made the decision.

CHAPTER 8

Conflict and Communication in International Development Projects

One major result of global political and economic integration must have been the steady destruction of the world's woodlands and forests, especially in the regions which were being newly integrated into that economy. . . . The rapid expansion of monocrop commodity production in the nineteenth and early twentieth centuries in the world's colonies and dependencies was one of the primary reasons for today's dangerous imbalance between the "First World" and "Third World."—*Global Deforestation and the Nineteenth-Century World Economy*, 1983.

BECAUSE the Bastar example offers vivid evidence, and because there are so many instances of conflict generated by similar attempts at technology transfer, we can reflect on the role that a deeper analysis of communication can play in international development. We do not mean simply that communication will result in less conflict, or that all interests can be reconciled. In fact, conflicts may represent a stage in the evolution of communication between governments, indigenous peoples, experts, and banks. The repetition of this kind of conflict all over the world invites other approaches to projects which are suggested below. But first it is necessary to weigh the significance of the Bastar project's termination.

Interpretation of the Bastar Project's Termination

A complete version of the history of the project lies in the memories and records of its actors and observers. Such a version could eventually be reconstructed if all the limitations on the use of certain materials and sources were removed. Because this will not occur for a long time, if ever, it is necessary to draw conclusions from the evidence offered in this book. We hope that the implications of what can be learned from the Bastar project will be transferred to other projects, and to other tribal people, incomplete though our understanding is at present.

First, what final interpretations of the rise and fall of this project are open to us? Without favoring any one interpretation, there appear to be three basic positions. The first interpretation is that the original project idea was poor and poorly developed, that the international planning system ultimately worked correctly, and that disaster was avoided. In this interpretation experts are blamed for the poverty of the project's ideas, and higher-level politicians and planners, including the Indian government, are credited with its termination. The unreliability of expertise, in this interpretation (which divorces social from forestry knowledge), is fortunately checked by struggles in the political arenas, including insistence of the tribal people.

The second interpretation is that the original project idea was good and its development satisfactory, but that there was external interference as well as competition with other investment project opportunities; furthermore, the supporting system failed, and all the work in Bastar resulted in waste. This interpretation sees the idea as being before its time, as too imaginative, and as one which politicians and planners failed to support through its initial and natural growth difficulties. The World Bank should have been more forceful, and the private sector should have made a commitment to Bastar: together, according to this interpretation, they could have succeeded with industrial forestry had the private and public sectors cooperated.

The third (mediating) interpretation is that the original idea was good, but its development was poor, or at least uncertain: people in the political and planning system became divided upon the merits of the project, and forces against it, at all levels, tipped the scales toward termination. Better luck, a better world economic climate, more political skill on the part of the World Bank and the forestry development corporation, along with other less tangible factors, would eventually have led to success. The poor project development is blamed upon forestry planners and consultants: had the project's development been good, the adverse externalities could have been overcome, including tribal resistance. A variant of this third position is that, although the original idea was poor, necessity would have forced its improvement in the long run—had history offered a long run. For example, one aspect of the project that might have been challenged, but was not, was the selection of an exotic species (*Pinus caribaea*). Many native Indian pines—for instance, chir pine—might have been suitable. In this sense, the five-years' work was a learning experience, necessary for a new undertaking based on poor ideas. All the work would have found its most suitable and adaptive form; eventually even the tribals would have been incorporated in industrial forestry in Bastar, with or without the private sector.

Ideas and Practice in International Development

Throughout the period in which the Bastar project was planned and conducted, and while government and World Bank officials were seeking to salvage the project during 1980 and 1981, other officials were engaged in the study and discussion of the alternative ideas for forestry development and its proper relation to tribal peoples. Such discussions are not at the heart of banking concerns, the way debt rescheduling and balance of payments are; some people in the development banking community, however, were pointing to the position of tribal peoples within prime resource areas, and to the requirement to communicate effectively with them in terms of their collective rights and futures.

The World Bank itself held significant discussions and announced a new policy for forestry during the Bastar project. Noting that 200 million people lived within and on the margins of forests in 1978, in countries in which the Bank had projects, the Bank decided some very fundamental change was required in its previously ad hoc approach to forestry.[1] Of seventeen projects in forestry between 1953 and 1976, thirteen had been oriented to various industries (e.g., paper), and four had been intended to benefit rural people in this group of 200 million. The World Bank made it clear that to change the distribution of its lending would "necessitate a radical change in its approach to forestry development. New concepts, technologies, and institutional approaches [would] have to be developed." The Bank's new forestry policy was to shift 60 percent of forestry loans to such projects as "environmental and protective forestry, rural development forestry, new plantations, agro-forestry, afforestation"; this would appear to stand the pattern of the preceding twenty-three years on its head.

To address this expanded horizon, the Bank stressed that many of the constraints within the forestry sector were sociological (population pressure, over-grazing, competition for land with farmers, firewood demand, and the tribal presence), but they could not be overlooked. Many of the constraints contained social conflicts. "Success in achieving these measures, however, can be both costly and politically unpopular." All the measures were viewed as long-term, yet the Bank pointed to the technical narrowness and lack of political influence of forestry institutions that had to carry out these new projects: they were viewed as too "self-contained".[2] (This was also an apt description of the MPFDC; yet it had been created, in part, by the Bank.)

At the outset, the 1978 policy paper acknowledged a conflict between the requirements of indigenous consumption and industrial uses of the forest and environmental conservation: "Some tribal groups live in the forests and are totally dependent on them. Others find, in forest products, part of their consumption needs, plus some items for processing and for trading with neighbouring groups."[3] Its projects, therefore, would have to address these conflicts, because they were likely to arise in the normal course of business.

An audit of the World Bank's projects in 1977 may partially explain why so little attention was paid to environmental research in the Bastar project. "The Bank staff, while generally conscientious in mitigating or avoiding adverse environmental consequences in their own projects, sometimes unwittingly overlook problems which seem to them peripheral."[4] This audit showed the World Bank unequipped to review the environmental impact of the large number of smaller projects (like Bastar); the Bank was doing "an increasingly good if somewhat sporadic job." Opposition within the Bank had, until that stage at least, stopped the inclusion of environmental and ecological considerations in the annual reviews of any member country's progress, but as time passed and ecologically minded people replaced older staff, said this study, conditions would improve. In praising the Bank's new forestry sector policy, this study said that because the World Bank is the "lender of last resort," borrowers cannot seek to minimize their environmental obligations elsewhere. This fact emphasizes the high responsibility the Bank holds in regard to ecological conservation.

Why communication between the Bastar project and tribal people was so poor requires another line of analysis. The tribals' primary position was mentioned in the 1978 forestry sector paper, and full analysis of the Bank's options regarding tribal people and economic development was being conducted even while the Bastar project was being terminated. This 1982 document referred to a moral imperative in which "the Bank accepts that entire tribes of human beings must not be sacrificed to the goal of economic development."[5] To achieve this, the issue of tribal rights in specific resources and territories had to be addressed by member governments and the Bank: "Subsoil (mineral), forestry, and space rights also may have to be reconciled between national legislation and traditional usufruct."[6]

Although there are suggestive signs of a moral imperative in the Bastar project, showing that special treatment had to be accorded to the tribal people, there is no evidence of any formal communication with them on these matters. This kind of communication was not completely foreign to the Bank, however: Perrett's study of funding for communication in such projects shows that investment had totaled $183 million during the 1970s. Although it accounted for only 2 percent of World Bank lending in 1979, this kind of funding addresses a fundamental issue in projects dependent for their success on whether beneficiaries participate or how they respond.[7] Even such modest communication support helps in a positive way in building the institutions of a project (including forestry projects); it also "helps to deal with negative behavior and attitudes, and prevent negative impact."[8]

Although the objections of the tribal people to the Bastar project became fundamental opposition, there was presumably a time before the project began in which significant communication with them was possible. Such communication had to address their rights in (and their uses of) the forest, as the Bank documents so clearly state. Since this project's success depended upon the initial and continuing response of the tribals, and its expansion intended that they should participate as workers even though they were not its primary beneficiaries, it is strange that the groundwork for such participation was never laid.

The World Bank was not alone in expressing an interest in these ideas. For example, agencies of the United States government and the United Nations held the same discussions during the same period. The U.S. Department of State held a national conference in 1978 on tropical deforestation. Following this conference, studies of the type conducted for the State Department by the University of Washington on U.S. corporations in tropical forestry were initiated. Weyerhaeuser Corporation's experience with caribbean pine and gmelina plantations in Indonesia was discussed along with the World Bank's forestry experience in Africa.[9] One conclusion of this national strategy was that

> the use and implications of *clear cutting in tropical forests* require research and analysis on an urgent basis—particularly in view of the expansion of interest in, and technology for, forest plantations and the economic use of naturally regenerated secondary species. In general, clear cutting should be applied only within the framework of a broad and sound strategy for long-term use and management of a forest area, or where the land is clearly suited to a higher economic or social use such as food production [emphasis in original]. [10]

Finally, during the terminal phase of the Bastar project, the United Nations' specialized agency, the Food and Agricultural Organization, was planning a series of meetings and studies on appropriate technology in forestry, the conservation and development of tropical forests, and the establishment of pulp and paper industries. One of these meetings on appropriate technology was held in India in 1981, and the FAO documents show that every difficulty faced by the Bastar project was discussed (although nowhere is Bastar, specifically mentioned). Improved hand tools, safety footwear, the use of draft animals, field preparation for accidents, and increasing the productivity of workers and machines were all discussed. Other FAO meetings discussed the macrosectoral problems of establishing a national industry in pulp and paper; how it should be protected and whether used machinery from developed countries could be transferred. Small-scale pulp mills in India (50–150 tons per day) were described as viable due to the special economic conditions prevailing: the experience of the International Finance Corporation, the World Bank, and PICOP (a World Bank project in the private sector in the Philippines) were discussed.[11] Every issue raised by the Bastar project was also discussed at the FAO in Rome during a multiagency expert meeting on conservation of tropical forests, but it is interesting that a project of the magnitude of the Bastar project, in which the FAO had been so long involved, disappeared from discussion in these reports.[12] Ultimately the year 1985 was designated by the United Nations as International Year of the Forest, with high level intergovernment meetings.

It is true that such meetings and reports constitute an industry on their own. The Brandt Commission estimated that in 1980 there were

6,000 international meetings on development issues in New York and Geneva alone. But one should not conclude that such activity bears no relation to actual development practice, and that it is thus irrelevant. On the contrary, ideas circulated in such reports can have progressive (or regressive) effects in investment projects and among member governments. To dismiss them as rhetorical window-dressing is to misunderstand their role. What is actually occurring through such studies and reports is the continual definition and redefinition of development problems (in this case, the problem of tropical forests) from the point of view of the key actors in prevailing institutions. But in pointing to the progressive potential of the circulation of ideas, one should not forget that during the formative stages of the Bastar project, the good ideas published in the Bank's 1978 forestry sector paper were already in circulation. Arguably there is a lag between the circulation of ideas and the acceptance of (some of) them; others are rejected, and still others are not contemplated seriously. The will and discipline to realize these ideas in action or in projects is the scarce resource. The success or difficulty in realizing ideas in projects, in turn influences their circulation and vitality. Ideas for theories and models, like practices in development projects, have their protagonists and antagonists within and without such institutions as the World Bank.

'The Public and Private Aspects of Tropical Forestry

There seem to be widely differing views of the cause of conversion of tropical forests, quite apart from its velocity. One view is represented by the University of Washington Study (Bethel et al., 1982) for the U.S. Department of State, that conversion is caused more by forest farmers and animal grazers than by transnational corporations seeking new resources.[13] Said this study, "Contrary to popularly-held beliefs U.S. multinational corporations are not major causes of tropical deforestation." In contrast with other private logging activities, it said that "U.S. forestry corporations are seldom involved in conversion."[14] A second view is that "logging is the main cause of degradation of tropical forests. It also earns more money from them than any other activity."[15] Caufield concluded (1984) that in Indonesia, Brazil, the Philippines, Papua New Guinea, and India commercial logging was the most important cause of deforestation. In this view, the focus is on corporations headquartered or owned in a number of countries, not just the United States. A third view is represented by Payer (1983), who says that the main engine of deforestation has been the drive for profitability of forestry corporations of the private sector. Multilateral agencies, in particular the World Bank, have often provided the access and initial support to forest projects that eventually benefit the private sector. In this view, the Bank is intensely interested in the overall legal framework that sets the terms for the forest exploitation. The Bank sees the poor people as killing the forest, whereas the corporations harvest the forest rationally to earn foreign exchange.[16] Payer does not believe the Bank when it says it acts merely as an honest broker between competing interests. But the forest farmers and even grazers have a different status, in Payer's view: the corporations cannot have a claim equal to those who dwell in and around the forest. The Bank's assistance to the former far outweighs its investment in the futures of the latter, says Payer. Yet it is the public sector's primary responsibility to consider the future of forest dwellers.

In the Bastar project, the expectation of the private sector's investment in addition to the World Bank's did not materialize. By 1972 the total nationalization of forest products by the government of Madhya Pradesh may have inhibited the private sector, not to speak of the many obvious and predictable logistical and management difficulties in Bastar. In this case, then, deforestation was planned and begun by the government, using public sector instruments (departments, corporations) for "the public good" or "the national interest." Half of the cost and most of the significant expertise were provided by the World Bank. As in other international development agencies, and private corporations, people within the World Bank are divided in their opinion regarding the public sector's ability to carry out natural resource planning and extraction. Some say the public sector is enfeebled by bureaucratic procedures, which take precedence over efficiency and the optimum use of personnel. Moreover, the public sector is routinely subject to direct political interference. Others disagree; the forests, like other natural resources, are a public good and a public property that should be developed only in the public interest by governments. In this view, a public forest development corporation is the appropriate instrument of a government, which can then fully regulate its behavior.

The fact is that the forestry development corporation, a creature spawned by the Forest Department of Madhya Pradesh and the World Bank, with Government of India approval, set about to behave essentially as a private-sector enterprise with the same goals of profitability. The department saw the corporation as a good way to capture more of the profitability of nationalized forests without having to turn them over to state revenue. (Note that in its second year of operations, the corporation paid the department a large sum as cost of a lease of land.) The Bank saw the corporation as a disciplined vehicle, more efficient than its parent department, and sealed off from the "grasping hand" of the department (which, after all, has many unprofitable undertakings it is bound to carry out). The standing assets of much of the forest were to be stripped, the value captured by the corporation (with spin-off benefits to private-sector resource users, if any), and much of the forest replaced with a single-tree plantation, whose use would be entirely dedicated to new industry. Once successful, the scale of operations could be greatly enlarged. All of the feasibility study was concentrated on the minimum starting size rather than on how big it could grow. Forest Department officials had already predicted seven and one-half times greater revenue within twenty-five years (Rs 6 billion, not the 1976 figure of Rs 800 million). The differences between the private and public sector's behavior—particularly in terms of the effect on tribal people—are hard to identify. In either case, they were not to plan and execute the expansion/investment if successful, just as they did not plan or execute the original feasibility study. It appears to have been fundamentally unimportant to tribals that the project was in the public sector; in fact, the distinction between the two, in this case, seems blurred.[17]

Communication Responsibilities of Multilateral Agencies

The speeches of Robert McNamara and A. W. Clausen, presidents of the World Bank, are full of references to the Bank's high responsibilities. Its head office staff and field officers refer to the same responsibilities. The Bank is, after all, the world's largest source of financial support for economic and social development of poor countries; it has a command of expertise which others do not, including many of its member-governments. Governments and peoples look up to the World Bank as a source of conservative and thorough analysis of development problems like tropical forestry. It is sometimes difficult to realize such responsibilities, but the Bank is nevertheless expected to try. In particular, one can suggest that multilateral agencies have "communication responsibilities."[18] These mean that member-governments and their peoples should be kept informed, and the Bank ensures that certain specialized publics are supplied with reports and news. These responsibilities vary in degree with different publics, but in general it is recognized that the Bank, like other multilateral agencies, should feel responsible for helping the rest of the world learn from its rich and costly experience, experience no others can replicate. If this is done, then surely there is a particular obligation to communicate with those who stand in the way, so to speak, of its projects and investments—those like the tribal people, who may either be its "beneficiaries" or its "overlooked." Also, surely, the Bank has a responsibility to contribute to the slowly accumulating fund of scientific knowledge, in forestry as in other fields, in proportion to the expertise and money it commands. This knowledge must be applied, more and more, as the cost of "safeguards" in international development go up and up.

In the Bastar case, there was no single scientific research center where the work was done: planning and scientific expertise came from Oxford, Bhopal, Washington, New Delhi, and Vancouver. But although the responsibility was diffused, it was held ultimately by the World Bank. Through its International Development Association (IDA), it loaned $4 million (53 percent of the total) and caused the Indian government to match these funds. These IDA funds have not been raised on commercial money markets, but from direct contributions made by member-governments: indeed, the replenishment of IDA funds has been a contentious issue among the Bank's member-governments during the 1980s. Members of the IDA like the Canadian or American governments in turn raise this money through taxation of common citizens. The use of these IDA funds thus reflects indirectly upon common citizens in donor countries. They would presumably not wish the World Bank to invest in projects of which they felt their own governments could not approve. National executive directors of the World Bank were presented with the recommendations for the Bastar project for this very reason.

Accountability is thus clearly established: the World Bank acts on behalf of many when it organizes a project, even a preliminary one, such as the Bastar project. It works with member-governments, on sovereign territory, and often defers to those governments even when their obligations are not fully met. Nonetheless, there is circulated within the World Bank a list of "unfulfilled covenants"—that is, goals or functions in specific projects which are not met or are significantly in arrears. The Bank's senior officers must regularly decide which unfulfilled covenant on this list is an issue over which the Bank will exercise its responsibility—that is, in which cases it is believed likely to succeed in obtaining completion by using various kinds of leverage.

In the case of the Bastar project the Bank's officials not only had extended the project for one year but also were preparing for the major investment. At the end of four years they sent in an FAO mission and Bank mission in quick succession to try to get the best advice, prepare a favorable investment proposal, and overcome obvious criticism of the project. This was done in the knowledge that one of the fundamental questions—the relation of tribal people to the present forests—had not yet been properly studied. What little evidence there was had been minimized by the corporation and department that would ultimately gain from the Bank's investment. Their weak preliminary sociological and environmental analysis would not have passed the scrutiny of some member-governments of the World Bank. Indeed, it seems not to have met the approval of the Government of India. But what if there had been no criticism or resistance in India? People associated with the Bastar project appear to have rejected criticism of it because they believed such criticism was maliciously motivated. What if the government had reinforced this attitude and rejected the same critical views, so that Bank officials had found a totally receptive environment for the project in 1981? How then would the World Bank determine its responsibility? And what then should that responsibility be?

This question of diffuse responsibility is not raised to press some narrow sectarian or protectionist claim, such as "The Bank should not fund projects overseas, using Canadian funds, which tend to hurt world trade in pulp and paper" simply because existing Canadian capacity in this industry is underutilized. Such narrow claims have already been made upon the Bank (e.g., by U.S. soya producers protesting palm oil projects in Asia). In the Bastar case, the project objectives were not being achieved. Even if they were not well-balanced objectives, the Bank was responsible for ensuring that they were fully met. It is important, therefore, to press the Bank to assert such original objectives, even if other key project institutions in a country are indifferent.

For $8 million very little useful science was created by the Bastar project. The project had by far the largest multipurpose forestry research fund in India in the 1970s, with an unprecedented amount of available foreign exchange. But the Bastar project results have had very limited circulation. Little research done in poor countries has held such a potential for interaction of local and international expertise, yet the resulting work has yielded little of significance to the large Indian scientific community, to the scientifically less-developed state of Madhya Pradesh, and particularly to the 1.84 million people of Bastar.

Anyone wishing to learn what the project uncovered would have great difficulty. The information is in Washington, Oxford, Vancouver, New Delhi—scattered—and with the forestry development corporation. Some of it is in the minds of people who will not return to Bastar. Many of the documents are locked away or are marked "not for public use." But they contain very little classified information that should not be published in scientific fora and consequently evaluated. Specific information that is commercially or nationally sensitive (the reason for restrictions) can very easily be omitted from publication: 90 percent of this information that the World Bank now regards as "classified" in these documents began as public information gathered by public servants at public expense and added to by expert consultants.

There is no good reason to restrict the use of most of this information: on the contrary, it may be in the Bank's interest to publish it, so that others may learn from the Bastar project and avoid repeating its mistakes. Surely the Bank's work is thus made easier, ensuring at least that other forest development projects are better informed and that the tribal people are more productively involved in these projects. The World Bank's own view of learning from mistakes is quite positive, and the accumulation of scientific knowledge subject to evaluation is thus essential to it: the 1981 review of project audits in eighty-seven projects showed 93 percent of the investments "remain worthwhile." In the view of the Bank, "mistakes, of which the Bank has its share are not often repeated. Subsequent projects build on earlier ones in the same sector."[19]

The secrecy surrounding this big project—which became essentially a research project—seems also to have raised suspicions that do the World Bank little good. Indirectly this suspicion hurts modern forestry, because people who do not understand these applied sciences will have less sympathy for them in the future. Thus, whether backed by the paramilitary support of a Forest Department or not, contract science of the Bastar project type must look to its future and to its interaction with the public scientific community. In some countries research work like the Bastar project is mandated by the state, and a public inquiry is sometimes held: the whole process results in a corpus of knowledge more or less open to scrutiny. Had this been the case, the results of the Bastar project would eventually have been useful to the tribals and other people in Bastar, even though the project was not planned in terms of its benefits to knowledge.

The Prior Status of Tribal People

In all of this, the status of the tribal people was extremely ambiguous. In one sense, they were continuously present—at the side of the road when jeeps whizzed by, at the weekly markets and timber auctions, and working in the forestry project itself. In another sense, they were largely absent—whether because they were uncommunicative themselves, or were ignored by others, or both. Their voice was everywhere muffled, except when they took a daring and dramatic step. If only the project had communicated with the tribals, some people assert, everything might have succeeded; yet others believe the tribals would eventually have had to communicate with the project. This ambiguity also resulted from the tribals' curious status in the very environment the project sought to transform. Archaeological evidence suggests they pre-date other settlers of Bastar, but their ancient presence has now become more or less a concession granted by the state. The project itself threatened the status of tribals, although it could and probably should have been the occasion to clarify and strengthen their rights, particularly in the forest.

In the history of tribal use of resources, there is no strong evidence of rights of ownership in the modern exclusionary sense. Every situation of use was the result of negotiation between interested parties. Of course, the overall authority in the matter of resources was the king. He, too, was open to negotiation, particularly in respect to settlement of disagreement over resources. Such negotiation was always conducted at the annual *durbar*, where political decisions were worked out and then widely communicated. This absence of clear and simple rights was ambiguous to outsiders as well. It also offered full scope for exploitation. The durbar, too, has been largely bypassed by government officials. It can be seen that diminution of tribal rights in the forests has run parallel to the gradual neutralization of tribal political institutions and processes.

The ambiguity has been, in part, semantic. The government has eroded its formal definition of the tribal presence in the forests of Bastar. First, tribal use of the forest was a "right." This right was then restricted to a "privilege." It was slowly transformed to a mere "concession" by 1963. From the tribal perspective, it could be construed that this constant diminution of their status in the forests has been equivalent to the sacrifice mentioned by the Bank. While their experience has been nothing like the genocide referred to by the Bank's report on tribal peoples, the Bastar tribals describe the change in their relation with the forest as a loss of their way of life. Such a loss would unalterably destroy their coherence as functioning social groups.

Finally, the ambiguity relates to the fact that the tribal people's knowledge of the forest and ability to manage it for their ends is both old and enduring, even if it is now becoming increasingly more limited by a larger population competing in scarcity. This very knowledge and capability, however, seems to have eluded the planners who were dreaming of the Ruhr of the East.

The Indian government finds itself in the contradictory position of responding in practice to the demands and vicissitudes of international economics by the sacrifice of local interests to the national interest (via a form of internal colonialism), while ideologically proclaiming the aims of social justice and protective tribal development. At the center of the contradiction lies the seemingly irresistible impulse to develop (read "expropriate") tribals' resources at the expense of tribal people. The greater the potential yield from this impulse, the greater the rhetoric.

On this basis, the failure of tribal development in India can be substantially explained. The overt reasons, as summarized by Jones from the reports of the Indian government itself over the last thirty years, fall into four main areas:

> Firstly the [protective] laws and [special tribal] programs have failed because of the power of the non-tribal landlords, money lenders and traders who control the tribal economies and local *panchayats* (councils). These groups in alliance with non-tribal government servants—development and revenue officers, administrators and magistrates—have been able to circumvent the laws and regulations and to divert development funds intended for tribals to their own use. Second, the development programs have failed because they have often been transferred without modification from the culturally and environmentally different plains areas and because their implementation has been left to poorly trained and culturally prejudiced non-tribal officers. Third, the programs have failed because they have not involved tribals in their own development. The use of the term "uplift" demonstrates the government's philosophy of development. Development is something done to tribals by non-tribals, not a process in which the tribals are actively involved and control. Fourth, . . . the funds allocated for tribal development have been totally inadequate for the immense task of providing the necessary infrastructure and inputs . . . [in fact] it seems that funds spent by the Government of India in tribal areas are considerably less than the value of the minerals and timber extracted from these areas.[20]

The underlying reason for this clearly discordant state of affairs, which not only fails to benefit tribal people but actually perpetrates among them severe social economic and cultural dislocation, is that the Indian government itself, whether at the national or state level, is one of the main beneficiaries of tribal exploitation.[21] This is recognized in official analyses of the situation. Given the immense value of natural resources in tribal areas, especially timber and minerals, on international as well as domestic markets, and the fact that political support for the Government of India derives fundamentally from those social classes which most profit from the exploitation of tribal people, it is hardly surprising that tribal development remains for the most part an unconscionable sham. From their inception right to the present time, it has been recognized that developmental program benefits for tribals "did not flow to the tribal communities. They only strengthened the exploitative elements."[22]

It may be perceived that such a characterization of tribal development in India is excessively negative, that these kinds of analyses form part of a worldwide corpus of polemical literature designed to thwart "progress" and "modernization." Considered especially suspect in this regard, social scientists and the anthropologists among them are often accused of exhibiting bleeding-heart sentimentalism and an exaggerated concern for human rights. These concerns are seen ultimately as self-interested obstructionism. There used to be an argument, for example, which still surfaces on occasion, that anthropologists were motivated for scientific purposes to encourage the reservation of tribal areas as zoos or laboratories in which to conduct their studies in pristine environments.

To take this argument seriously, it may be assumed, is to be persuaded by caricature. Yet something of its force is nonetheless evoked even in the thinking of many technologically oriented development experts. Reporting on the feasibility of the Bastar project, the Sandwell company stated:

> In the simplest terms possible, the dilemma facing the Government of India with respect to its tribal people is finding a way to modernize tribal lifestyles in accordance with the rest of the country without total sacrifice of their traditional culture. To attempt to maintain present tribal lifestyles without change . . . is futile.[23]

Clearly, a scientific posture is presumed to exist which advocates no change, which, in short, is antidevelopment. Such an interpretation is indeed cast in the simplest terms. This, among social scientists at least, is not the case. What is futile is to attempt tribal development with only a rhetorical effort made to prepare and involve local populations in the inevitable process of change—which is a fact long recognized by social science. The more profound futility has to do with the political-economic stake a government may have in maintaining tribal underdevelopment, in order to maximize the revenues obtainable from the de jure expropriation of resources traditionally held in de facto ownership by tribal communities. In this case, it may be that the only real possibility of development of and for tribal people is attendant upon a radical restructuring of nontribal society.

In our introduction we spoke of an alternative. We suggested that genuine tribal development could evolve through a process of communication regarding the human ecological considerations intrinsic to economic change. The character and human use of the forests is definitely changing, and nontribals and tribals alike have grasped this fact. Tribals' engagement in modern forestry schemes, including industrial ones, does not have to lead to their sacrifice. Indeed, it can lead to their relative empowerment and allow them to conserve those features of life they define to be crucial. We are not conveying here, by innuendo or direct statement, that anyone seriously would wish the tribals sacrificed; that is, would wish them to disappear. We have been struck by the fact that no one, even among those prejudiced against tribals, has thought their disappearance would be a good thing. How, then, are tribals to communicate with others and be communicated with? What can be said to them? How should their interests be heard? Clearly the answers lie with forests: if tribals do gain control of and have uninterrupted responsibility for forests, they will begin to take other necessary steps to adapt to modern forestry rather than simply to reject it. They have a deep and ancient knowledge of trees, and they can learn everything modern science could teach them.

A language, or code, must evolve for this communication. There must be a shared context. The code can be constructed from the meanings and uses of the forest, but the process of construction will be slow because of past disagreements. Using tribal dialects in Bastar, the shared tribal Gond language, and the official language Hindi, a working understanding can be achieved. The realization that the forest represents a common future, not exclusive to any party, will provide the impetus for communication. The media for this communication are the traditional grounds of tribal/nontribal encounter: the weekly markets, the annual durbar, and village meetings. An All-India Radio broadcast station has been sitting underutilized in Jagdalpur for years. During the project it broadcast ninety minutes daily in local languages. The tribals must also set their own agenda for this communication, and the process must always be open to negotiation. Other delicate subjects, too, may eventually be considered, but the starting point is the forest.

Throughout this book, there has been reference to the term "social forestry," used alike by foresters in the field and by distant economic planners. The implication is that forests can be used more to satisfy current household needs and less for industrial production. Reviews of this idea, which is variously called village forests, rural forests, panchayat forests, community forests, and farm forests, have shown that the forestry literature in India has a long tradition of exhortations toward its achievement in practice. The earliest written proposals go back to Dietrich Brandis, the first Inspector General of Forests brought to India in the 1860s. Every subsequent proposal recognizes the need to have secure forests for firewood and other purposes on a sustained yield basis. Having reviewed all of these schemes, Taylor has concluded that the problem addressed in each one is "the conflict between forestry and agriculture for land."[24] Some imaginative experiments of this type begun in the 1930s in Bastar suffered from the same conflict: until now, the value of some other crops has been greater than the value of firewood.

But what is the ultimate meaning of social forestry? It seems to be an empty term in forestry vocabulary, vacant like some of the land on which these new forests are supposed to grow. Its opposite term, "production forestry," refers to existing intact forests protected or reserved by forestry departments and intended for industry and revenue. But is production forestry not equally social? Does it not speak of social relations and invoke social ideologies regarding work and technology? Or, conversely, is it true that social forestry is not productive, as the distinction suggests? If so, has a shallow meaning of "production" flourished so quickly, and an empty meaning of "social"? In this case, "social" conveys no sense of obligation or control; its apparent neutrality avoids the politics of rights in forests and trees and the unequal economics of their use. Perhaps that is why it has gained currency so swiftly.

From the perspective of planners working in the Bank and the Indian government, it can be seen, however, that establishing the legitimacy of social forestry has been like establishing an island in an unfriendly sea. The social referent, characteristically ignored by most foresters, engineers, and economists in the Bastar project, has become a point from which to resist the unsocial process of planning and through which to press for significant changes.

Governments and international agencies have shown genuine readiness to face the need for community forests when they have been dealing with the problem of tropical forestry. India has been no less alert to this, and social forestry plans have been made in almost every state. But in the midst of this optimism, careful analysis has pointed to the shortcomings of such plans, because most land allocated for social forestry has, to date, been uncultivable. Said Kulkarni, "social forestry schemes can never meet the needs of the rural population for firewood, fodder and other minor forest products" unless better quality land held by forest departments is also assigned to these purposes. "The concept of social forestry developed by the forest departments needs a radical change."[25] The difficulty here, observed Gadgil, is that "we must press for the poetic content of our development plans to be genuinely translated into practice. . . . This is not achieved by declaring that it shall be so. The social forces have to be moulded to ensure that it will be so."[26]

CHAPTER 9

Epilogue

In 1985 Walter Huber returned to Bastar to observe informally the character of the area's development since the demise of the pine project. What follows is a short account of some of the "changes" in Bastar during those five years. These so-called changes were, in fact, more like continuities—reaffirming and enlarging upon the enduring deficits of sacrificial development.

Obvious at once was the recently fortified wall of secrecy, the "bamboo curtain" placed before the interested observer in the 1980s. It had become necessary to seek permission for *any* visits beyond the district capital of Jagdalpur. This restriction did not originate with the Government of India, but rather with the state government of Madhya Pradesh. The explanation proffered by district authorities involved an ill-defined controversy over a BBC film project centered on life in a Muria *gotul* (youth dormitory). With little in the way of justification, the restriction was extended to all foreigners. Huber was no exception. Although a certain freedom of movement was allowed, it became apparent that the bamboo curtain was serving to conceal that Bastar was still being seen, and treated, as the El Dorado of India. As we stated in our conclusion, little seems to have been learned from the termination of the Bastar pine project.

Although not much remains of the project itself, the new buildings built for the MPFDC have been staffed by mining-development personnel, whose task it is to administer and implement a dolomite-extraction project in the Kurundi area—the same area, it will be recalled, that was targeted for the pine trials. The dolomite project has provoked the same kind of negative local reaction as did the earlier forestry project. In this case, as well, the native forests of the area are slated for elimination, with no more than the (by-now) usual offer of wage labor to compensate the forest-dependent tribal populations. It appears that direct tribal protest has forced the suspension of the dolomite project. According to a protribal activist interviewed in August 1985, a large contingent of tribal people had demonstrated before the visiting Madhya Pradesh Minister concerned with mining. The tribal group met the Minister at the Jagdalpur airport, each person bearing some forest product essential to his livelihood which would be eliminated if the dolomite project were to proceed. The Minister was reported to have been very receptive to this demonstration.

Although situated close (near Barsur) to the same site earlier selected for one of the alternate locations of the forestry project's pulp mill, the 600-megawatt Bodhghat Dam Hydroelectric Project on the Indravati River is not likely to be abandoned. Work at this site was well underway in 1985, with the estimated date of project completion being 1991. The dam will not provide any irrigation services, nor will any tribal people be employed in the project except as manual laborers. The primary forest area to be submerged is estimated at 32,270 hectares. This includes thirty-nine villages with a 90 percent tribal population of approximately 6,360.[1] As of August 1985 the Madhya Pradesh Forest Department had not approved the clearance of the forest areas, but this was regarded by dam officials as a mere formality.[2] The unilateral displacement of several thousand tribal inhabitants of the affected area was also taken as a matter of course. But by May 1987 the Central Government had still not approved the project.

Two further dam projects have been cleared through the planning stage. These are both located downstream from Bodhghat, one at Bhopalpatnam and the other at Inchampalli at the confluence of the Indravati and Godavari Rivers. Environmental analyst H. K. Divekar has evaluated the projects:

> The watershed of all . . . three projects is almost entirely habitated [sic] by tribals . . . [whose] villages are scattered in the entire watershed area. . . . With estimated submersions of over 1.7 lakhs [170,000] ha forests . . . , the consequential encroachments by the tribals into the interior . . . watersheds which are already under pressure will be a grave threat to the very existence of forests in Bastar.[3]

The Abujhmar area is the only remaining "true wild biosphere in peninsular India."[4] It will also be affected by these dam projects and, as explained above, has now experienced the beginnings of infrastructural development, consisting of stretches of deeply penetrating roads and the establishment of administrative subcenters.

Along with these relatively remote undertakings, a number of industrial projects have taken shape in the Jagdalpur area, including a large cement factory to which opposition (mainly by the urban-centered ecology lobby) has been generated. From the controversies surrounding all the post-pine developments, it is obvious that the earlier polarization concerning resource exploitation in Bastar has not only continued but has, in fact, intensified.

This increase in official development activities has swelled the influx of already large numbers of government and contract employees to the district, as well as of small-scale (or perhaps not so small-scale) "entrepreneurs," who have seen the glint of El Dorado. Among the latter are some who have taken up such unofficial activities as widespread tin smuggling, reportedly in collusion with some "high connections" in the state Mining Department.[5] The journalist who filed the tin-smuggling reports in 1985 was found murdered at Kondagaon in Bastar some two weeks later.[6] The bamboo curtain in and around Bastar district is not designed only to keep out foreigners, nor is it without potentially lethal consequences for those who attempt its removal. Not so long ago, a king of Bastar ended up in analogous circumstances.

Over the last five years, India generally has witnessed a rapid growth of interest in environmental problems. Indeed, one may discern the start of an environmental movement in the country. In a lecture given in 1984 under the auspices of the Indian Council of Social Science Research, Anil Agarwal, director of the Center for Science and Environment, New Delhi, detailed some of the particulars of this nascent movement:

> The hundreds of [voluntary] field-level groups in the country today taking a keen interest in environmental issues and their experiences and interests are extremely diverse: while some are interested in preventing deforestation, there are others only interested in afforestation. There are many who want to prevent the construction of one dam or another. There are others who want to prevent water pollution. There is the famous Chipko movement in the U.P.

Himalayas, probably the oldest and most famous of all the groups, which has played a major role in bringing the issue of deforestation to the fore of public opinion. And now there is its counterpart in the south, the Apikko Movement in the Western Ghats of Karnataka. Dams like the Silent Valley and Bedthi have already been stopped because of strong people's protests and now the well known social worker Baba Amte, who has never been involved in any campaign all his life, is leading a major campaign against the proposed Bhopalpatnam and Inchampalli dams on the borders of M.P., Andhra Pradesh and Maharashtra.[7]

In Agarwal's analysis, such activities are in response to a major transformation and destruction of nature in India, in turn resulting from two intense pressures on the country's natural resources:

> The first, generated by population growth and thus increased demand for biomass resources, has been widely talked about. The poor often get blamed for the destruction of the environment. But the second set of pressures, generated by modernisation, industrialization and the general penetration of the cash economy, are seldom talked about. . . . Now, if in the name of economic development, any human activity results in the destruction of an ecological space, or in its transformation which benefits the more powerful groups in society, then those who were earlier dependent on that space will suffer. Development in this case leads to displacement and dispossession and will inevitably raise questions of social justice and conflict. The experience of microlevel groups shows clearly again that it is rare to find a case in which environmental destruction does not go hand in hand with social injustice, almost like two sides of the same coin.[8]

An example of the growth of voluntary field-level groups is the case of Kishore Bharati near Bhopal. In 1982, relates a founder, they visited Bastar because of the notoriety the district had achieved during the forestry project. In Anil Sadgopal's own words:

> Three years ago [1982], in a small study in the Bastar district in Madhya Pradesh, we asked some people this question: Which forces are responsible for the large-scale felling of forests in the district? Of course, the Chief Conservator of Forests said it was the Adivasis, the tribals, who were encroaching upon the forests near the villages. They were burning fuelwood, building houses with the wood, stealing bamboo, and taking more than the allowed headload of timber. And we found, to our surprise, that a

Hyderabad-based company was making a certain kind of steel for which it needed coal. To make the coal it had undertaken a large scale contract, using wood from the forests of Bastar. We found that the amount of wood this company was using for making steel was more than the total amount of fuelwood used by the Adivasis in that district; yet this fact will never be revealed to you by the forest authorities.[9]

This brief epilogue is perhaps best viewed as a footnote to the foregoing text. It would be redundant at this point to draw any further conclusions concerning the ill-fated Bastar pine project. It is evident, however, that recent events indicate a politicized awareness among indigenous groups which will lead to ever-increasing protest against and resistance to development projects indifferent to local needs. It is difficult not to be pessimistic about the future of Bastar as one of the last natural resource frontiers in India—perhaps in the world. The Bastar pattern has been repeated too often in too many places. But we hope that the analysis of information and the recommendations presented in tracing the pattern will help in the continuing efforts to find an equitable balance between socioeconomic development and ecological well-being. These efforts must come from many quarters—and many times over.

Critiques of the sort we offer here have not been ignored by everyone within the Bank. In 1985 a number of analysts published reviews under the important title, "Putting People First." Although Bastar was not mentioned, the broad issues of deforestation, environmental degradation, social forestry, and indigenous people were addressed in studies by Noronha, Spears, and Cernea, and alternative approaches were proposed.[10] But the pressure from outside the Bank continued: in 1986 the formation of a nongovernment coalition of groups called the Tropical Forests Working Group began in Washington. The group's guidelines for financing forest projects called, in 1987, for project-by-project vigilance by the U.S. Executive Director at the World Bank. Saying that most earlier projects had "been particularly notorious for failing to achieve sustained productivity," stringent preconditions were proposed by the Group before projects proceed in tropical moist forest areas.

Also we find today that the World Bank is advised again by the Overseas Development Council of the United States to remember its mandate—to deal with poverty (as expressed in the World Bank forestry sector policy of 1978), and to find projects that strengthen the ecological relations of the poor. "Future energy loans could not only give more emphasis to renewables (particularly fuelwoods, charcoal, and crop residues) but also to establish pricing policies that discourage wasteful harvesting of forests and give incentives to smaller farmers to participate in tree planting and conservation. Power projects that displace small farmers or indigenous minorities could go beyond compensation and more broadly establish the rights to compensation and resettlement."[11]

Meanwhile, the Brundtland Commission on the environment and development was drafting its final report. How to respond to these pressures was discussed at the Bank during 1986 and early 1987, particularly in light of its current experience in countries like India where major hydroelectric and irrigation projects were being stalled due to land-use conflict which involved, among others, tribal people. The question was, apparently, one of proper compensation for loss of habitual forested environments. Then just before the publication of the Brundtland Commission's report, the Bank announced in May 1987 the formation of a new Environment Department with the equivalent of one hundred full-time staff (compared to the current seventeen persons). One of the other environmental initiatives announced simultaneously by the Bank was a program to promote the preservation of tropical forests. These announcements occurred in the midst of dramatic personnel restructuring at the Bank, brought about by calls for a more efficient operation.

Dispossession in Bastar has long been raising questions of rights to social justice, and conflict as a recurring phenomenon has taken different forms. The struggle over forests in Bastar did not stop when the pine project was terminated. In early 1987 reliable reports were received about groups of tribal women in Jagdalpur and Kondagaon confronting government administrators over the allegedly illegal removal of forest products by officials of the Forest Department (and other departments). In effect, they were turning back upon the accusers the very accusations so long leveled at tribal people. They were also bringing to Bastar the technique of public confrontation used successfully by women in the Chipko Andolan movement of the Himalayan foothills, during the early 1970s. As the South African novelist Nadine Gordimer has said: "There are many forms of resistance not recognized in orthodox strategy."

Notes

Chapter 1. Introduction: Bastar and the Problem of Tropical Forests

1. James S. Bethel, *The Role of U.S. Multinational Corporations in Commercial Forestry Operations in the Tropics* (Seattle: University of Washington, College of Forest Resources, report submitted to the Department of State, 1982).

2. J. P. Landy, *Tropical Forest Resources* (Nairobi: United Nations FAO in conjunction with United Nations Environmental Program, 1982).

3. Norman Myers, "Deforestation in the Tropics: Who Gains, Who Loses?," in *Where Have All the Flowers Gone? Deforestation in the Third World*, eds. V. H. Sutlive et al. (Williamsburg, Va.: College of William and Mary, 1981), p. 12.

4. Norman Myers, *The Primary Source* (New York: Norton, 1984), pp. 178–85; see also Nicholas Guppy, "Tropical Deforestation: A Global View," *Foreign Affairs* (Spring 1984), pp. 928–65.

5. Food and Agriculture Organization (hereafter cited as FAO), *Forest Resources of Tropical Asia* (Rome, 1981), p. 179.

6. Catherine Caufield, *In the Rainforest* (New York: Knopf, 1984), p. 80.

7. Bethel, *The Role of U.S. Multinational Corporations*, p. 33.

8. Robert I. Rotberg and Theodore K. Rabb, eds.,*Climate and History: Studies in Interdisciplinary History* (Princeton: Princeton University Press, 1981). On the "edge effect," see Thomas Lovejoy et al., "Ecosystem Decay of Amazon Forest Remnants," in *Extinctions*, ed. M. H. Nitecki (Chicago: University of Chicago Press, 1984), pp. 331–54.

9. International Development Association (hereafter cited as IDA), *Report and Recommendations of the President of the Executive Directors on a Proposed Credit to the Government of India for Forestry Technical Assistance* (Washington, D.C.: World Bank, October 1975); see also *Report and Recommendations . . . for the Madhya*

Pradesh Forestry Technical Assistance Project No. P-1733-IN (Washington, D.C.: World Bank, December 1975).

10. See, for example, S. B. Chaudhuri, *Civil Disturbances During the British Rule in India, 1765–1851* (Calcutta: World Press, 1955).

11. Kathleen Gough, "Indian Peasant Uprisings," *Economic and Political Weekly*, 9 (August 1974): 393.

12. C. von Furer-Haimendorf, *The Tribes of India: The Struggle for Survival* (Berkeley, Los Angeles, and London: University of California Press, 1982), p. 313. The Indian nationalist rejection of special treatment and protection of tribal peoples has been carried over into the contemporary period. The following statement on the definition of the term *tribe*, by a "seasoned" Indian administrator, is a typical example: "I am not in favour of any definitions based on ethnographic or anthropological considerations . . . and we should not do anything that would result in perpetuating the differences between them [the tribals] and the rest of the populations." See T. B. Naik, "What Is a Tribe: Conflicting Definitions," in *Applied Anthropology in India*, ed. L. P. Vidyarthi (Allahabad: Kitab Mahal, 1968), p. 96. More seriously (in some parts of India), there have also been recent large-scale protests and violent demonstrations against special measures for tribals.

13. C. von Furer-Haimendorf, "The Position of the Tribal Population of Modern India," in *India and Ceylon: Unity and Diversity*, ed. Philip Mason (London: Oxford University Press, 1967), p. 211.

14. C. von Furer-Haimendorf, *Tribes of India*, pp. 57–77, 79–96.

15. Paul Hockings, "Review of the Tribes of India," *American Anthropologist*, 86, no. 2(1984): 468.

16. Wilbert E. Moore, *Social Change* (Englewood Cliffs, N.J.: Prentice-Hall, 1963), p. 89.

Chapter 2. The Tribals and Their Kingdom

1. Government of India, *Census of India 1981* (Provisional Population Total, Series 11, Madhya Pradesh, Paper no. 1, Indian Administrative Services, Director of Census Operations, New Delhi, 1981).

2. K. V. Sundaram, R. P. Misra, and V. L. S. Prakasarao, *Spatial Planning for a Tribal Region: A Case Study of Bastar District, Madhya Pradesh* (University of Mysore: Institute of Development Studies, 1972), p. 11.

3. Edward Jay, *A Tribal Village of Middle India*, Anthropological Survey of India, Memoir no. 21 (Calcutta, 1970), p. 39.

4. Summarized in C. von Furer-Haimendorf, *The Gonds of Andhra Pradesh* (New Delhi: Vikas, 1979), pp. 1–15.

5. Figures here are derived from the 1961 Census of India. In subsequent enumerations no figures are given for individual tribes. For a complete account see Walter Huber, *From Millennia to the Millennium: An Anthropological History of Bastar State* (Master's thesis, University of British Columbia, 1984).

6. C. von Furer-Haimendorf, "A Central Indian Tribal People: The Raj Gonds", in *South Asia: Seven Community Profiles*, ed. Clarence Maloney (New York: Holt, Rinehart and Winston, 1974), p. 206.

7. There exists a long-standing anthropological debate on the definition of the tribe and, in India, the unresolved question as to whether, whatever the definition, there are peoples who can be so described. The issue is further complicated by the presence of castes in India, so that the question is enlarged to include tribes, castes, and peasants. It is impossible in a footnote to resolve this issue but a few comments may help to clarify it. On a descriptive basis, the anthropological tradition of calling some Indian groups *tribes* rather than *castes* derives from identifying as tribes those peoples who "almost always live in relatively isolated hill or jungle areas, follow a form of shifting cultivation, hunting and gathering, or pastoralism, quite frequently speak a language that is different from that spoken in the surrounding plains, and participate less completely in the higher forms of Hindu religious ceremonial." See Stephen Tyler, *India: An Anthropological Perspective* (California: Goodyear Publishing Company, 1973), p. 179. On a sociological basis, the differentiation is much more subtle. Very simply put, tribes are egalitarian whereas castes are hierarchical. Using economic criteria, however, most tribes in India, and in Bastar, must be considered peasants.

8. T. Popoff, *The Muriya and Tallur Mutte: A Study of the Concept of the Earth Among the Muriya Gonds of Bastar District, India* (Ph.D. diss., University of Sussex, 1980), p. 139.

9. Wilfred V. Grigson, *The Maria Gonds of Bastar*, reissued with Supplement, 1949 (London: Oxford University Press, 1938), p. 197.

10. It is not likely that the Hill Maria will much longer be allowed to maintain their self-elected isolation, nor their strong attachment to swidden cultivation. They are among the last tribal groups in India who have as yet to undergo the "modernization" process—a process, as has been well documented, fraught with ambivalence, ambiguity, and, almost invariably, a good deal of trauma for tribal peoples. Exactly when this process will begin in the remote Abujhmar (the Hill Maria region) is difficult to predict, although the timing will probably

coincide with the conclusion of natural resource surveys presently being conducted. Perhaps the most trenchant and informed treatment of tribal modernization, in both its positive and (mostly) negative aspects, is found in C. von Furer-Haimendorf, *The Tribes of India: The Struggle for Survival* (Berkeley, Los Angeles, and London: University of California Press, 1982).

11. FAO/World Bank Cooperative Program Investment Center, *Draft Report of the India, Madhya Pradesh Commercial Forestry Development Project Preparation Mission*, Annex 12 (Rome, 27 April 1981), p. 8.

12. Sunderam, Misra, and Prakasarao, *Spatial Planning*, p. 11.

13. Madhya Pradesh State Forestry Development Corporation (hereafter cited as MPFDC), *Introducing M.P. Forestry Technical Assistance Project, Bastar, India*, General Bulletin (Bhopal, December 1978), p. 3.

14. For example, "Bastar, in its unique virginity, offers ample scope for large-scale industrialisation and colonisation." See Syed Ashfaq Ali, *Tribal Demography in Madhya Pradesh*, Appendix no. 9, "Bastar Can Relieve Paper Shortage" (Bhopal: Jai Bharat Publishing House, 1973), p. 318.

15. Grigson, *Maria Gonds*, p. 3.

16. Quoted ibid., p. 13.

17. Ibid., p. 14.

18. See R. Temple, *Report on the Administration of the Central Provinces for the Year 1862*, Reprint (Nagpur: Government Press, 1923).

19. Robin Jeffrey, *People, Princes and Paramount Power: Society and Politics in the Indian Princely States* (Delhi: Oxford University Press, 1978), pp. 10–11.

20. R. Temple, *Report 1862*, pp. 80–81.

Chapter 3. Forest-Tribe Relations

1. Verrier Elwin, ed., *A New Deal for Tribal India* (New Delhi: Ministry of Home Affairs, 1963), p. 51.

2. Stebbing's classic studies of forestry policy and practice do not include princely states like Bastar, but since practices of forestry there followed those of British India, these volumes are invaluable: E. P. Stebbing, *The Forests of India*, vols. 1, 2, 3 (London: Bodley Head, 1922, 1923, 1926), vol. 4 (London: Oxford University Press, 1962). See also papers by J. F. Richards, M. B. McAlpine, and R. P. Tucker in *Global Deforestation and the Nineteenth-Century World Economy*, eds. R. P. Tucker and J. F. Richards (Durham: Duke University Press, 1983).

3. Edward Thompson, *The Making of the Indian Princes* (London: Oxford University Press, 1944), p. 271.

4. Wilfred V. Grigson, *The Maria Gonds of Bastar*, reissued with Supplement, 1949 (London: Oxford University Press, 1938), p. 10.

5. D. N. Tewari, *An Intensive Forest Management Plan for Barsur Industrial Catchment*, Madhya Pradesh Forest Department (Jagdalpur, 1974), p. 77.

6. B. P. Standen, *Confidential No. 60*, Central Provinces Administration, Political and Military Department, Jagdalpur Records Room, Bastar, 1910, para. 10.

7. C. von Furer-Haimendorf, *The Tribes of India: The Struggle for Survival* (Berkeley, Los Angeles, and London: University of California Press, 1982), p. 80.

8. Ibid., p. 48.

9. G. S. Arora and N. E. Reynolds, *India's Tribal Population and Its Social and Economic Development* (New Delhi: Ford Foundation, n.d. ca. 1975), pp. 29–35.

10. Quoted in Elwin, *A New Deal*, p. 52.

11. Ibid., p. 71.

12. R. Joshi, "Bastar: The Politics of the Timber Trade," *Economic and Political Weekly* (Bombay), 13 November 1976, pp. 1785–86.

13. Steve Jones, "Tribal Underdevelopment in India," *Development and Change*, 9 (1978): 48.

14. For analysis of the behavior induced by this relationship elsewhere, see Jack Bilmes, "Why Do Thai Villagers Break the Wood Laws?" *Human Organization* (Summer 1980): pp. 186–89.

15. Tensions around regulation, violation, and punishment are important measures of competing uses of Bastar's forests. A proposal by Robert Anderson to have the frequency of violations, sanctions, or exemptions carefully studied in the tehsils marked for the pine plantations, in the context of the tribal study, was not approved. Such measures, then, lie buried in the files or memories of forest officials and tribals. Interestingly, an excellent model of such a study existed, published at the commencement of the Bastar project: E. P. Thompson's *Whigs and Hunters: The Origin of the Black Act* (London: Allen Lane, 1975). This work is a rich account of the effects of legislation passed in 1723 which severely curtailed historic uses made by "the public" of the large Windsor forest and Berkshire forests of England. As in Bastar, the removal of wood or trees, hunting of deer, and access to all other forest products (e.g., turf, fish, grass) were put under official superintendents who were licensed to engage in a predatory relation to these forests, to the exclusion of others. Thompson shows how the act was used to intimidate and subjugate violators, and how the severity of the act provoked groups of poor violators to challenge it throughout the eighteenth century. Confrontations over deer hunting were particularly violent. Customary and historic rights (including the right to gather firewood) were curtailed or

eliminated, and the forest became the preserve of the privileged few. Said Thompson, "The forest conflict was, in origin, a conflict between users and exploiters" (p. 245).

16. V. G. Kohli, *Proposals for Social Forestry in Bastar District*, Intensive Management Division, no. 1, Jagdalpur (Bastar, 1976), p. vi.

17. S. S. Srivastava, *Questionnaire of the Forest Nistar Policy Committee, Madhya Pradesh, with General and Explanatory Notes* (Rewa: Government Regional Press, 1959), p. 106.

18. Elwin, *A New Deal*, pp. 54–55.

19. For an account of over 250 years (1590–1868) of regulation and conflict in Japan's most famous forests, see Conrad Totman, *The Origins of Japan's Modern Forests: The Case of Akita* (Honolulu: University of Hawaii Press, 1985).

Chapter 4. Plans for Industrial Forestry

1. M. S. Tomar and G. Saxena, eds., *Souvenir of the Madhya Pradesh Forest Department* (Bhopal: Government Central Press, 1976).

2. E. Van Es and S. C. Joshi, "Growing Stock Estimates from Aerial Photographs in Bastar, Madhya Pradesh," *Commonwealth Forestry Review*, (March 1974): 30–38.

3. Marketing and Research Corporation of India, *A Survey of India's Export Potential of Wood and Wood Products* (New Delhi, 1970).

4. Ibid., p. 7.

5. Ibid., p. 11.

6. D. N. Tewari and Eladio Susaeta, *Formulation and Economic Assessment of an Intensive Forestry Project for the Bastar Region of Madhya Pradesh* (New Delhi: Ford Foundation, 1973), p. 9.

7. Ibid.

8. Ibid., p. 45.

9. D. N. Tewari, *An Intensive Forestry Management Plan for Barsur Industrial Catchment* (Jagdalpur: Forest Department of Madhya Pradesh, 1974), p. xxi.

10. Ibid., p. 19.

11. Ibid., p. 77.

12. Ibid., p. 20.

13. Ibid., p. 19.

14. Ibid., p. 10.

15. Ibid., p. 11.

16. IDA, *Report and Recommendations of the President to the Executive Directors on a Proposed Credit to India for the Madhya Pradesh Forestry Technical Assistance Project*, No. P-1733-IN (Washington, D.C.: World Bank, 16 December 1975), p. 10.

17. Ibid., p. 15.

18. Ibid., pp. 13–14.

19. Ibid., p. 13.

Chapter 5. The Project and the Tribal Study

1. Hence, this description does not conform precisely to Warren C. Baum, *The Project Cycle* (Washington, D.C.: World Bank, 1982).

2. MPFDC, *Introducing M.P. Forestry Technical Assistance Project*, Bastar, India, General Bulletin 12 (January 1978), p. 15.

3. FAO, *Forest News for Asia and the Pacific*, Bangkok, 2, no. 3 (August 1978): 44.

4. B. J. W. Greig and L. E. P. Foster, "Fomes Annosus in the Pine Plantations of Jamaica," *Commonwealth Forestry Review* (December 1982): 269–75.

5. MPFDC, *Introducing M.P. Forestry Technical Assistance Project*, p. 4.

6. Rajesh Pant et al., *Pulping and Bleaching of Mixed Hardwoods from the Central Indian Forests (Bastar)* (New Delhi: Hindustan Paper Corporation and FAO, 1979).

7. Sandwell Management Consultants Ltd., *Bastar Pulp and Paper Mill Investment Feasibility Study* (Vancouver, 1979).

8. Ibid., p. 20.

9. IDA, *Report and Recommendations* No. P-1733-IN (Washington, D.C.: World Bank, 16 December 1975), p. 13.

10. D. Hajra, *The Dorla of Bastar*, Anthropological Survey of India, Memoir no. 17 (Calcutta, 1960); Edward Jay, *A Tribal Village of Middle India*, Memoir no. 21 (Calcutta, 1970); K. N. Thusu, *The Dhurwa of Bastar*, Anthropological Survey of India, Memoir no. 16 (Calcutta, 1965).

11. Personal communication, 1 December 1978.

12. V. G. Kohli, *Proposals for Social Forestry in Bastar District*, Jagdalpur Indian Forest Service, Intensive Management Division, November 1976. Also, V. G. Kohli, *Socio Economic Study of Tribals of Bastar District*, Indian Forest Service, Intensive Management Division (Jagdalpur, December 1977).

13. Kohli, *Proposals*, p. 13.

14. See IDA, *Forestry Sector Policy Paper* (Washington, D.C.: World Bank, 1978).

15. *Visit of the Parliamentary Committee on the Welfare of Scheduled Castes and*

Scheduled Tribes to Bastar District: A Brief on the Points for Discussion with Local Officials, 1977.

16. Personal communication, 26 June 1979.

17. Personal communication, 15 December 1980.

18. "Centre to review pine project in Bastar," *Times of India* (Bombay), 14 October 1981.

19. FAO/World Bank Cooperative Program Investment Center, *Draft Report of the India, Madhya Pradesh Commercial Forestry Development Project Preparation Mission*, Annex 12 (Rome, 27 April 1981), p. 13.

20. FAO/World Bank, *Draft Report of Mission*, p. 3.

21. *Times of India* (Bombay), 14 October 1981.

22. Personal communications, 6 April 1982, and 3 March 1983.

23. Tribal Research and Development Institute, *Impact of Bastar Forestry Project on Tribal Economy: An Economic Study* (Bhopal: Tribal and Harijan Welfare Department, Government of Madhya Pradesh, n.d., ca. 1980). Note that a later report of the same title (no date) was issued by the Department of Tribal and Harijan Welfare. This may be another version of the report assessed here, because the sample size of the survey is smaller (216 households, of which 187 were tribal and 29 nontribal, in eleven villages). This version is richer in detail regarding the difference in forest-dependence between agricultural and nonagricultural villages: it particularly emphasizes the economic difficulties of villages (e.g., Dhourai) which are situated close to the eucalyptus plantation created in the 1960s. See Bharat Dogra, "The World Bank vs. the People of Bastar," *The Ecologist*, 15, 1/2, (1985): 44–58.

24. S. Solanki, Minister of Forests, Panchayat and Social Welfare of Community Development, "Message," in *Souvenir*, eds. M. S. Tomar and G. Saxena (Bhopal: Government Central Press, 1976), p. v.

25. S. C. Shukla, Chief Minister of Madhya Pradesh, "Message," in *Souvenir*, p. i.

26. V. G. Kohli, *Proposals for Social Forestry*, pp. 3–8.

27. C. von Furer-Haimendorf, *The Tribes of India: The Struggle for Survival* (Berkeley, Los Angeles, and London: University of California Press, 1982), pp. 201–3.

Chapter 6. Market Trends, Alternative Investments, Unresolved Issues

1. We are grateful to Daniel Breck of Woodbridge, Reed and Associates of Vancouver for assistance with this analysis.

2. James Bethel and Adelina I. Tseng, "Developing Countries as Markets for Forest Products," in *World Trade in Forest Products*, ed. Gerald F. Schreuder (Seattle: University of Washington Press, 1986), pp. 287–315.

3.Bethel and Tseng, "Developing Countries as Markets," pp. 287–315.

4. IDA, *Forestry Sector Policy Paper* (Washington, D.C.: World Bank, February 1978), p. 34.

5. Ibid., p. 9.

6. United States General Accounting Office, *Changes Needed in U.S. Assistance to Deter Deforestation in Developing Countries*, GAO/ID-82-50 (Washington, D.C., 16 September 1982), pp. 4, 23. This report incorporates the responses of the Departments of State and the Treasury, as well as USAID and the U.S. Forest Service. Assessment is made of the FAO, among others. The pressure to lend did not wane: between 1977 and 1986 the Bank financed $1.341 billion worth of forestry projects. "Tropical Forests Working Group Newsletter," (Washington, D.C., vol. 1, no. 2, June 1987), p. 1.

7. IDA, *Forestry Sector Policy Paper*, p. 50.

8. United States General Accounting Office, *Changes Needed to Deter Deforestation*, p. 23.

9. See also, *Blowing in the Wind: Deforestation and Long-range Implications* (Williamsburg, Va: College of William and Mary, Studies in Third World Societies, 1981).

10. O.P. Saxena, "Tropical Pines: An Alternative to Long Fibre Raw Material," in *Souvenir*, eds. M. S. Tomar and G. Saxena (Bhopal: Government Central Press, 1976), pp. 43–46.

11. Certain other varieties of *P. caribaea*, including *hondurensis, bahamensis, caribaea*, were tried in Bastar. These varieties are collectively referred to as *Pinus caribaea Morelet*. The first published analysis of *P. caribaea* was made in a report to the Government of Honduras by a visiting Indian Forest Service expert (E. D. M. Hopper) in 1887.

12. Government of India, *Pre-investment Survey of Forest Resources: Industrial Plantations and Species Performance Trials*, IND/100/4 (New Delhi: UN Special Fund-FAO Project for Government of India, 1967).

13. Saxena, "Tropical Pines," in *Souvenir*, p. 45.

14. G. L. Gibson, R. D. Barnes, and J. Berrington, "Provenance Productivity in *Pinus caribaea* and Its Interaction with Environment"; and G. L. Gibson, R. D. Barnes, and J. Berrington, "Flowering and Its Interaction with Environment in Provenance Trials of *Pinus caribaea*," *Commonwealth Forestry Review*, 62, no. 2 (1983): 93–106, and 62, no. 4 (1983): 251–64. For the history of work at Oxford on

pines, see R. H. Kemp, "International Provenance Research on Central American Pines," *Commonwealth Forestry Review*, 52, no. 1 (1973): 55–66.

15. A. Greaves, *Description of Seed Sources and Collections for Provenances of Pinus caribaea* (Oxford: Commonwealth Forestry Institute, 1978).

16. R. A. Plumptre, *Pinus caribaea*, vol. 2, *Wood Properties* (Oxford: Commonwealth Forestry Institute, 1984), p. 11.

17. Ibid., p. 106.

18. FAO/World Bank Cooperative Program Investment Center, *Draft Report of the India, Madhya Pradesh Commercial Forestry Development Project Preparation Mission*, Annex 12 (Rome, 27 April 1981), p. 65.

19. M. R. Sivaraman, "The Role of Forests in a Developing Economy," in *Souvenir*, p. 13.

20. R. C. Ghosh, "Socio-economic effects and constraints in forest management," in *socio-economic Effects and Constraints in Tropical Forest Management*, ed E. G. Hallsworth (Toronto: John Wiley & Sons, 1982), p. 25.

21. Government of India Planning Commission, *Report of the Fuel Wood Study Committee* (New Delhi, 1982).

22. R. C. Ghosh, "Socio-economic effects," p. 29.

23. Raymond Noronha, "Why Is It so Difficult to Grow Fuelwood?," *Unasylva*, 23, no. 131 (1981).

24. *Report of the National Commission on Agriculture*, vol. 9 (New Delhi: Government of India, 1976), p. 359.

25. FAO/World Bank Cooperative Program Investment Center, *Draft Report of the India, Madhya Pradesh Commercial Forestry Development Project Preparation Mission*, Annex 12 (Rome, 27 April 1981), pp. 10–11.

26. IDA, World Bank, Annex 5 (October 1975), p. 2.

27. IDA, World Bank News Release no. 82/13 (Washington, D.C., 17 September 1981).

28. *Report of the National Commission on Agriculture*, 9: 381.

29. Greaves, *Description of Pinus caribaea*, p. 7.

30. FAO/World Bank, *Draft Report of Mission*, p. 11.

31. M. K. Dalvi, "Foreword," in *Socio-economic Effects*, ed. Hallsworth, pp. viii, ix. (This is the Inspector General's introductory address to the 1981 international conference on tropical forest management in Dehra Dun.)

32. B. D. Sharma, *Industrial Complexes and Their Tribal Hinterlands: Forests, Tribal Economy, and Regional Development*, Occasional Papers on Tribal Development, nos. 16 and 26 (New Delhi: Ministry of Home Affairs, 1978).

33. Susanna Hecht, "Deforestation in the Amazonian Basin: Magnitude, Dynamics and Soil Resource Effects," in *Where Have All the Flowers Gone?*

Deforestation in the Third World (Williamsburg, Va.: College of William and Mary, Studies in Third World Societies, 1981); see also Christopher Uhl, Carl Jordan, and Rafael Herrara, "Amazon Forest Management for Wood Production," in *Socio-economic Effects and Constraints*, ed. Hallsworth, pp. 150–51.

34. Walter Fernandes and Sharad Kulkarni, eds., *Towards a New Forest Policy: People's Rights and Environmental Needs* (New Delhi: Indian Social Institute, 1983), p. 84.

35. Center for Science and Environment, *The State of India's Environment, 1982* (New Delhi, 1982).

36. "Inaugural Address by The Hon. Rao Birendra Singh, Minister of Agriculture, India," in FAO, *Appropriate Technology in Forestry*, Report of the Consultation Held in 1981 in New Delhi and Dehra Dun (Rome, 1981), p. 8. In the contention between state and federal government interests, and between the public and private sectors, India does not stand alone. Canadian forestry contends with the same struggle. Regarding the American situation, see also, Roger A. Sedjo, *Investment in Forestry: Resources, Land Use, and Public Policy* (Boulder: Westview Press, 1985).

Chapter 7. The Risk of Tribal Resistance and Retaliation

1. IDA, *Report and Recommendations*, No. P-1733-IN (Washington, D.C.: World Bank, 16 December 1975), p. 18.

2. Kirit Doshi, "Firing in Bailadila" (trans. from Hindi), *Link* (Bombay), and *Nai Duniya* (Bhopal), 18 May 1978.

3. Ram Sharan Joshi, "Impact of Industrialization on Tribals: A Case Study of Bailadila, Bastar," *National Labour Institute Bulletin* (August 1978), pp. 1–14.

4. Sharad Chandra Verma, "Disaster For Bastar," *Inside/Outside* (Bombay, April–May 1979), pp. 32–36.

5. Ibid., p. 35.

6. C. von Furer-Haimendorf, *The Tribes of India: The Struggle for Survival* (Berkeley, Los Angeles, and London: University of California Press, 1982), p. 80.

7. FAO, *Draft Report of the India, Madhya Pradesh Commercial Forestry Project Preparation Mission*, Annex 12 (Rome, 1981), p. 14.

8. K. L. Pandey, *Report on the Disturbances Which Took Place at Jagdalpur on the 25th and 26th March 1966* (Bhopal: Government Central Press, 1967), p. 21.

9. Wilfred V. Grigson, *The Maria Gonds of Bastar* (London: Oxford University Press, 1938), p. 14.

10. Ibid., pp. 14–15.

11. Ibid.

12. Ibid.

13. B. P. Standen, *Confidential No. 60*, Central Provinces Administration, Political and Military Department, Jagdalpur Records Room, Bastar, 1910, p. 7.

14. Pandey, *Report on the Disturbances*, p. 27.

15. Pravir Chandra Bhanj Deo, *I Pravir: The Adivasi God* (Raipur, 1965), p. 52.

16. Pandey, *Report on the Disturbances*, p. 27.

17. *Statesman* (Calcutta), 23 November 1960.

18. *Statesman* (Calcutta), 22 December 1960.

19. Quoted in Bhanj Deo, *I Pravir*, p. 10.

20. Ibid., p. 161.

21. Pandey, *Report on the Disturbances*, p. 35.

22. Verrier Elwin, *The Muria and Their Ghotul* (Bombay: Oxford University Press, 1947), p. 183.

23. Pandey, *Report on the Disturbances*, p. 36.

24. Ibid., p. 107.

25. Ibid., pp. 107–109.

26. Grigson, *The Maria Gonds*, p. 76.

27. *Times of India* (Bombay), 14 October 1981.

28. *Indian Express* (New Delhi), 7 February 1982.

29. *Hindu* (Madras), 14 February 1982.

Chapter 8. Conflict and Communication

1. IDA, *Forestry Sector Policy Paper* (Washington, D.C.: World Bank, 1978), p. 9.

2. Ibid., pp. 34–35.

3. Ibid., p. 14.

4. International Institute for Environment and Development, *Multilateral Aid and the Environment*, report of work in progress (London, September 1977), p. 22.

5. Robert Goodland, *Tribal Peoples and Economic Development: Human Ecologic Considerations* (Washington, D.C.: World Bank, May 1982), p. 15.

6. Ibid.

7. Heli E. Perrett, *Using Communication Support in Projects: The World Bank's Experience* (Washington, D.C.: World Bank, 1982).

8. Ibid., p. 16.

9. United States Department of State, *Proceedings of the U.S. Strategy Conference on Tropical Deforestation* (Washington, D.C., October 1978).

10. Ibid., p. 11.

11. Regarding the relation of PICOP, the World Bank, the Soriano family, and International Paper Company, see Cheryl Payer, *The World Bank: A Critical Analysis* (New York: Monthly Review Press, 1982), pp. 302–3.

12. FAO, *Appropriate Technology in Forestry*, Report of the Consultation Held in 1981 in New Delhi and Dehra Dun (Rome, 1982); FAO, *Conservation and Development of Tropical Forest Resources*, Report on Expert Meeting (Rome, 1982); FAO, *Establishing Pulp and Paper Mills: A Guide for Developing Countries*, Proceedings of the FAO Advisory Committee on Pulp and Paper, 1981–83 (Rome, 1983). See also FAO, *Tropical Forest Plan of Action* (Rome, 1985).

13. James S. Bethel et al., *The Role of U.S. Multinational Corporations in the Tropics* (Seattle: University of Washington, College of Forest Resources, report submitted to the Department of State, 1982).

14. Ibid., p. 18.

15. Catherine Caufield, *In the Rainforest* (New York: Knopf, 1984), p. 150. See also Nicholas Guppy, "Tropical Deforestation: A Global View," *Foreign Affairs* (Spring 1984), pp. 928–65.

16. Payer, *The World Bank*, pp. 299–300.

17. This ambiguous relationship is dealt with in S. I. Benn and G. F. Gaus, eds., *Public and Private in Social Life* (New York: St. Martin's Press, 1983).

18. In 1980 international conferences studied the communication responsibilities of the international agricultural research centers (IARCs), all of which "belong" to a consultative group coordinated and supervised by the World Bank. Indirectly the communication responsibilities of institutions like the World Bank, which underwrite the cost of the IARCs, were also considered. This included even the contentious issue of communication with those farmers who actually use the technologies these centers create or assemble and then transfer to participating governments. Any simple, direct responsibility was avoided. Instead, research and financing institutions discussed the diffuse, complementary, and supplementary responsibilies with which they sought to augment sovereign governments and their own programs. See International Rice Research Institute, *Communication Responsibilities of the International Agricultural Research Centers* (Los Banos, 1980).

19. Warren C. Baum, *The Project Cycle* (Washington, D.C.: World Bank, 1982), p. 24.

20. Steve Jones, "Tribal Underdevelopment in India," *Development and Change*, 9 (1978): 47–50. Citing the 1973 *Annual Report, Commission for*

Scheduled Castes and Scheduled Tribes, p. 395, Jones points out that the net revenue from exploitation of tribal forests in the Central Tribal Belt, including Bastar (assuming that tribal forests comprise 50% of the total), was Rs 243 million in 1969–1970. In the same year, the special tribal program expenditure was only Rs 109 million, that is, tribal expenditures were only 44.8% of revenues from tribal forests. The benefits of such an arrangement are clear. Observers say this ratio of revenue to expenditure was similar throughout the period of the Bastar project.

21. Jones, "Tribal Underdevelopment," p. 48.

22. Ajit Raizada, *Tribal Development in Madhya Pradesh: A Planning Perspective* (New Delhi: Inter-India Publications, 1984), p. 40.

23. Sandwell Management Consultants Ltd., *Bastar Pulp and Paper Mill Feasibility Study* (Vancouver, 1979), p. 20.

24. George Taylor, "The Forestry/Agriculture Interface: Some Lessons from Indian Forest Policy," *Commonwealth Forestry Review*, 60, no. 1 (1981): 50.

25. Sharad Kulkarni, "The Forest Policy and Forest Bill: A Critique and Suggestions for Change," in *Towards a New Forest Policy: People's Rights and Environmental Needs*, eds. Walter Fernandes and Sharad Kulkarni (New Delhi: Indian Social Institute, 1983), p. 99.

26. Madhav Gadgil, "Forestry with a Social Purpose," in *Towards a New Forest Policy*, eds. Fernandes and Kulkarni, pp. 113, 121.

Chapter 9. Epilogue

1. H. K. Divekar, "Environmental Consequences of Hydro-electric Projects in Bastar District, Central India," manuscript (Bombay Natural History Society, 1984), p.4. See also the observations of the Commissioner of Bastar and Chairman of its Tribal Development Authority, J. S. Kapanee, "A Brief Note About the Progress and Problems of Development Activities in Bastar Division" (Bastar, October 1984).

2. Personal communication, 19 August 1985.

3. Divekar, "Environmental Consequences," pp. 9–10.

4. Ibid., p. 7.

5. *Madhya Pradesh Chronicle* (Raipur), 8 June 1985.

6. *Indian Express* (New Delhi), 27 July, 1985.

7. Anil Agarwal, "Beyond Pretty Trees and Tigers: The Role of Ecological Destruction in the Emerging Patterns of Poverty and People's Protests," Fifth

Vikram Sarabhai Memorial Lecture, Indian Council of Social Research (New Delhi, 1984), p. 2.

8. Ibid., pp. 9–10.

9. *Sunday Herald* (Bangalore), 21 July 1985.

10. Cernea, Michael M., *Putting People First: Sociological Variables in Rural Development* (New York: Oxford University Press [for the World Bank], 1985).

11. Sheldon Annis, "The Shifting Grounds of Poverty Lending at the World Bank," in *Between Two Worlds: The World Bank's Next Decade*, ed. Richard Feinberg (Washington, D.C.: The Overseas Development Council, 1986), p. 107.

Bibliography

Baum, Warren C. *The Project Cycle*. Washington, D.C.: The World Bank, 1982.

Blowing in the Wind: Deforestation and Long-range Implications. Williamsburg, Va.: College of William and Mary, Studies in Third World Societies, 1980.

Caufield, Catherine. *In the Rainforest*. New York: Knopf, 1984.

Center for Sciences and Environment. *The State of India's Environment, 1982*. New Delhi, 1982.

Cernea, Michael. *Putting People First: Sociological Variables in Rural Development*. New York: Oxford University Press (for the World Bank), 1985.

Chaudhuri, Buddhadeb. *Tribal Development in India: Problems and Prospects*. Delhi: Inter-India Publications, 1982.

Dogra, Bharat. "The World Bank vs. the People of Bastar." *The Ecologist* 15, no. 1/2 (1985): 44–48.

Elwin, Verrier. *The Muria and Their Ghotul*. Bombay: Oxford University Press, 1947.

Elwin, Verrier, ed. *A New Deal for Tribal India*. New Delhi: Ministry of Home Affairs, 1963.

Fernandes, Walter, and Sharad Kulkarni, eds. *Towards a New Forest Policy: People's Rights and Environmental Needs*. New Delhi: Indian Social Institute, 1983.

Food and Agriculture Organization. *Conservation and Development of Tropical Forest Resources*. Report on Expert Meeting. Rome, 1982.

Food and Agriculture Organization. *Tropical Forest Plan of Action*. Rome, 1985.

Goodland, Robert. *Tribal Peoples and Economic Development: Human Ecologic Considerations*. Washington, D.C.: World Bank, May 1982.

Grigson, Wilfred V. *The Maria Gonds of Bastar*. Reissued with Supplement, 1949. London: Oxford University Press, 1938.

155

Guppy, Nicholas. "Tropical Deforestation: A Global View." *Foreign Affairs*. Spring 1984.

Hajra, D. *The Dorla of Bastar*. Anthropological Survey of India. Memoir no. 17. Calcutta, 1960.

Hallsworth, E. G., ed. *Socio-economic Effects and Constraints in Tropical Forest Management*. Toronto: John Wiley & Sons, 1982.

Huber, Walter. "From Millennia to the Millennium: An Anthropological History of Bastar State." Master's thesis, Vancouver: University of British Columbia, 1984.

International Development Association. *Forestry Sector Policy Paper*. Washington, D.C.: World Bank, February 1978.

Jay, Edward. *A Tribal Village of Middle India*. Anthropological Survey of India. Memoir no. 21. Calcutta, 1970.

Jeffrey, Robin. *People, Princes and Paramount Power: Society and Politics in the Indian Princely States*. Delhi: Oxford University Press, 1978.

Jones, Steve. "Tribal Underdevelopment in India." *Development and Change* 9 (1978).

Joshi, Ram Sharan. "Impact of Industrialization on Tribals: A Case Study of Bailadila, Bastar." *National Labour Institute Bulletin*. August 1978.

Myers, Norman. *The Primary Source*. New York: Norton, 1984.

Pandey, K. L. *Report on the Disturbances which took place at Jagdalpur on the 25th and 26th March 1966*. Bhopal: Government Central Press, 1967.

Plumptre, R. A. *Pinus caribaea: Vol 2, Wood Properties*. Oxford: Commonwealth Forestry Institute, 1984.

Popoff, T. "The Muriya and Tallur Mutte: A Study of the Concept of the Earth Among the Muriya Gonds of Bastar District, India." Ph.D dissertation, University of Sussex, 1980.

Schreuder, Gerald F., ed. *World Trade in Forest Products*. Seattle: University of Washington Press, 1986.

Sharma, B. D. *Industrial Complexes and Their Tribal Hinterlands: Forests, Tribal Economy, and Regional Development*. Occasional Papers on Tribal Development, nos. 16, 26. New Delhi: Ministry of Home Affairs, 1978.

Thusu, K. N. *The Dhurwa of Bastar*. Anthropological Survey of India. Memoir no. 16. Calcutta, 1965.

Tyler, Stephen. *India: An Anthropological Perspective*. Pacific Palisades, Calif.: Goodyear Publishing Company, 1973.

von Furer-Haimendorf, C. *The Tribes of India: The Struggle for Survival*. Berkeley, Los Angeles, and London: University of California Press, 1982.

Index

157

The Authors

Robert S. ANDERSON and WALTER HUBER both have long-standing interests in India.

Anderson first went to India at the age of 19, and studied there as an undergraduate and graduate student in Madras, Calcutta and Bombay. He received his Ph.D in anthropology (1971) from the University of Chicago and has taught at McGill and the University of British Columbia. He was also responsible for a Quaker post war reconstruction project in Bangladesh in 1972–73. He is now associate professor in the Department of Communication at Simon Fraser University, Burnaby, Canada. He reports he now is also responsible for a piece of classic raincoast cedar forest, and feels an unexpected connection with the forest dwellers of Bastar.

Huber has spent many years travelling and studying in South Asia since 1969 and has developed a primary focus on its tribal peoples. Huber's undergraduate and graduate degrees are from the University of British Columbia: a B.A. (1974) and M.A. (1984) both in anthropology. He recently completed a project on behalf of an aboriginal organization seeking reform of Canada's Indian Act Legislation. He currently works as a consulting anthropologist, and is teaching in Tokyo.